PICKING
AND
CHOOSING

ESSAYS ON PROSE

ALSO BY CAROLYN KIZER

Poetry
The Ungrateful Garden
Knock Upon Silence
Midnight Was My Cry
Yin
Mermaids In The Basement
The Nearness Of You

Translation
Carrying Over: Translations from the
Chinese, Urdu, Macedonian,
Yiddish, and French African

Essays
Proses: On Poems & Poets

Editions
The Essential John Clare
One Hundred Women Poets (forthcoming)

for Brad and Mary Jo,
fond Regards,
Carolyn Kizer

PICKING AND
CHOOSING
ESSAYS ON PROSE

BY

CAROLYN KIZER

August '98

EWU
P·R·E·S·S
Eastern Washington University Press
Cheney, Washington

Cover Art: Untitled, by Mathew Weaver, © 1995

Artwork for sections and chapter heads from linocuts and murals
by Rubén Trejo, © 1995.

Kizer, Carolyn.
    Picking and choosing : essays on prose / by Carolyn Kizer.
        p.   cm.
    ISBN 0-910055-25-4
    1. American prose literature—History and criticism. 2.
English prose literature—History and criticism. 3. Japanese
fiction—History and criticism. 4. Women and literature. I. Title.
PS364.K59   1995
818'.08—dc20
                                                    95-33603
                                                        CIP

Acknowledgments

The *New York Times Book Review* printed "Becoming a Heroine: Rachel Brownstein," "What Women Really Do Not Want: Elizabeth Janeway," "The Women We Feared to Become: Alice Adams," "The Education of Ilka Weissnix: Lore Segal," "Two Women Terrified: Eleanor Clark," "Mrs. Lessing's Nightmare: Doris Lessing," "How He Saved His Skin: John Jewett,"* "The Man Nobody Knew: Paul Scott," "In the Skin of a Lion: Michael Ondaatje."

*In somewhat different form.

The review of Ivy Compton-Burnett's biography appeared in the *San Jose Mercury News*.

The reviews of Renata Adler's novel *Pitch Dark* and Ross Terrill's biography of Madam Mao Zedong appeared in the *Washington Post Book World*.

"Reading Aloud to Children" was printed in the *New York Times*.

"Commencement Address: On Failure" was given at Eastern Washington University in Cheney.

DELOS printed "Donald Keene and Japanese Fiction" and "A Japanese Family Saga."

"Fictional Space: John Keeble" appeared in *Northwest Review*.

for   Barbara   and   Maxine
        Thompson   Kumin

PICKING AND CHOOSING:
Essays on Prose

Contents

Section I

WOMEN
AS
HEROINES

Becoming a Heroine:
Rachel Brownstein

Haven't you speculated on the effect that your reading—particularly during your early and adolescent years—has had on your life? Even in this unromantic time (for the death of romance seems to be one legacy of sexual freedom) we wonder if literate young women don't graduate from daydreams about a blend of Huck Finn and Holden Caulfield to a man who is an amalgam of the Msrs. Heathcliff, Rochester and Darcy. I feel reasonably confident of this statement because, Reader, I married him. (The fact that manic-depressives, gloomy and handsome, make lousy husbands was not borne in upon me until far too late.)

Now comes Rachel Brownstein's splendid book, to assert these connections between literature and life. Like the very best of feminist criticism, it tends to confirm what we have suspected in the privacy of our own heads, though believing that we alone nourished these notions. However, Ms. Brownstein's book, as the title indicates, focuses on how women learn to view themselves, rather than dealing with our unrealistic dreams of the hero who will rescue us from the banalities of home-life, homework and housework. I can hardly wait for her sequel.

Of course, the aim and end of the woman-centered novel has been, until modern times, marriage. The hero is viewed as the vehicle of her escape from her family, the validation of her individuality, and the ultimate reward for virtue, whether it be the obsession with virginity of the earliest novels, or the sturdy independence of later heroines: sharp-tongued Elizabeth, or plain, and plain-spoken, Jane. What a comfort these non-beautiful heroines have been to generations of girl bookworms with misted spectacles! The authors who emphasized what my mother referred to as "inner beauty"—so much more important in the long run than mere prettiness—were women themselves, it goes without saying.

Male authors knew better.

Ms. Brownstein does not fail to point out that men read novels and have fantasies, as well as women. However, girls, "enjoined from thinking about becoming generals and emperors, tend to live more in novels than boys do, and to live longer in them." Engagingly, she illustrates this thesis with an account of her own life and reading. Hooray for her! says this reader, yearning for women scholars openly to drop the assumption of detachment and objectivity which has blanketed conventional criticism for so long, encouraging the pretense that scholars belong to some meta-human species, as organless as angels, sans malice, sans envy, sans normal aspiration. It's a pity that, just as Ms. Brownstein reaches the time of decision in her own life, she chickens out on us. Whom did she marry, and why did she marry? And then what happened? Oh, it's relatively easy for this reviewer to complain, who divorced Heathcliff some decades ago, but one can't help regretting the smooth transition into a more conventional type of critical analysis, brilliant though much of it is.

She is trenchant and provocative in her analysis of *Clarissa, Villette*—that strange, perverse novel wherein we are defied to identify with Lucy, the narrator-protagonist, and do so anyway!—*The Egoist, Daniel Deronda, The Portrait of a Lady*, and *Mrs. Dalloway*, but it is in considering the novels of Jane Austen that Ms. Brownstein sings her most pellucid arias. For this rabid Janeite, convinced that there were no new insights to be gained in thinking about *Pride and Prejudice,* it is painful to forbear from quoting pp. 102 - 132 in their entirety. These inadequate snippets will have to serve: "For all her superiority, gender ties Elizabeth Bennet to the heroine's plot. It will not do for her to spend her forever-after in Olympian chastity with her father, gossiping about the world and its wives . . . Elizabeth can realize herself only by getting married; in other words, she must do with her life what her mother did with hers, and what her mother wishes her to do." "Disdain for her mother and what she represents must be in some part abated if Elizabeth is to be more than her father's daughter, and distaste for the collusion against her mother that her father had forced upon her is an important beginning of the process. In preparation for leaguing forever with the decorous Mr. Darcy, Elizabeth identifies in Mr. Bennet's behavior 'that continued breach of conjugal obligation and decorum . . . in exposing his wife to the contempt of his own children.'" Elizabeth explains to her father that she no longer hates Darcy but loves him. "Mr. Bennet repairs to his library, ruefully declaring himself at the disposal of those who might want his remaining unmarried daughters . . . He has been diminished."

He has "effectively given up his favorite daughter by assuming she is like most women after all. Because she has decided to marry, Elizabeth seems to her father no longer the special creature she was when she was altogether his, altogether virgin, although different from her mother and other women . . . meanwhile, she has found him to be a less reliable moral authority than she had imagined." Ms. Brownstein, rather like the late Professor Bradley, eminent Shakespearean scholar, goes on to speculate about the future life of the characters after the novel concludes. She imagines that Mr. Bennet will visit the Darcys often, "evidently without his wife." My girlish fantasies along these lines were less sanguine: How on earth was the formidably vulgar Mrs. Bennet to be prevented from imposing herself on the Darcy *ménâge?*

I shuddered at the vision of Mr. D. giving Mrs. B. the old freezola when she makes a particularly egregious gaffe, while poor Elizabeth silently writhes . . . But these idle speculations only testify to the durability of Miss Austen, that great spinster-enchantress. In Rachel Brownstein she has found a worthy exegete.

Becoming A Heroine: Reading About Women in Novels, by Rachel M. Brownstein. New York, Viking Press, 1982.

What Women Really Do Not Want: Elizabeth Janeway

E lizabeth Janeway has done us a number of significant favors in recent years, as she has gone deeper and deeper into the historic situation of women in society, with particular reference to woman's place today. She has informed us of the leadership of women in other times, from the medieval period when women were left to tend to the multifarious duties and responsibilities of running principalities, estates, manors and farms, while the males were off—sometimes for years—running wars, to the settlement of the American West, when women functioned, perforce, as full working partners of their men. She has told us how many of our notions of woman's place are of relatively recent vintage—many of them dating from the Victorian era, the '20s, even the '50s—when they have been seen as calcified by ancient tradition. She has pointed out that the nuclear family is fast becoming a myth of the Moral Majority, and that its destruction is not reversible by forcing women out of jobs, banning abortion, praying in the schools or denying sex information to the young.

And Janeway is not simply airing *her* prejudices; her learning is abundant, and her statistics impressive: "Back in 1950, six married men were breadwinners for every married woman; now it's less than two." "The once average family of four (both parents present) where only the father works has shrunk to an unprecedented low: in 1976 a mere 7 percent of all families. At the same date, nearly 20 percent of American families were headed by women." The vast majority of women work because they must, not because they long for a color TV. Among other fascinating figures, we learn that *only half* of divorced or separated women are paid the child support to which their children are entitled. And women, married or single, must worry about their young ones while at work, and worry about their jobs when they must take time off to aid their children, and are denied, for the most part, the support of adequate child-care facilities to relieve their burdens and reduce their frantic anxiety.

When I was a girl, I was always thrilled when I saw the label of the International Ladies' Garment Worker's Union sewn into my clothes. The women who made my blouses and skirts had their own union! It was only a few years ago that I met a retired union official, vacationing in Mexico, who told me that she had been, and still was, the only female union official in the history of the ILGWU, and that her life with her colleagues had been one of intense frustration, as her proposals were habitually ignored or voted down. Janeway confirms that in occupations where women are in a substantial majority, all the unions are dominated and run by men.

It is difficult to think of another woman writing today who is more trenchant and illuminating in her commentary on our situation. Occasionally Janeway is so urgent in her need to inform us that she slides into jargon words such as "meaningful," "nurturing," "nitty-gritty," and "input"—the shorthand of a woman in a hurry. Since I am attempting, right now, to avoid the use of the phrase "role model" in describing her, I see the problem.

Cross Sections is her collection of essays from the last 10 years, "a decade of change." Two major essays are a history of the women's movement, which is as good as you can find

8

anywhere, and a piece on American women's literature she wrote in 1977 for the *Harvard Guide to Contemporary American Writing*, recently revised, owing to the outpouring of women's writing since that time. But in mid-1974, when Janeway began to search out American women writers publishing since 1945, there was not a single guide to aid her. So what we have here is an original survey, admirably comprehensive, of our recent work, supplemented by later reading. However, this means, as Janeway points out, that "we have no standard canon and no accepted measures for judging this writing." Good! The reader is invited to disagree and to supplement the list of writers discussed. On the whole, it is a shrewd and thoughtful analysis, from her comment on the parallel Gertrude Stein draws, in *Wars I Have Seen* (1945), between the situation of women and that of an occupied country, to her description of Elizabeth Hardwick's critical and imaginative intelligence, "of such a high order that one feels it stands outside of history."

I enjoyed very much the sight of Janeway, this intelligent woman who has been preoccupied with other matters, turning her full attention to poetry: Louise Bogan! Muriel Rukeyser! H.D.! Mona Van Duyn! What a good time she has, reading them and speculating about them; she has an acute appreciation of the insight that a fine poem can convey in a phrase.

But I must resist the temptation to dwell on Janeway's literary essays, when she serves up real meat and potatoes in the chapters on work and sex. Here are two comments on woman as achiever: "If women hesitate to take prompt and decisive action," it isn't so much the famous fear of success as it is "sheer, learned self-doubt," based on the unpredictability of our situation, as we wait for instructions from a higher authority. "One ends by simply not daring to care or to think ahead of what may be." Which leads us "to the well-known finding that women and members of powerless inferior groups and classes have trouble delaying the satisfaction of their desires. . . . If you can't tell what's going to happen to you, if your judgment of events has been rendered suspect even in your own mind, how can you possibly waste time trying to imagine a future?" (Reading these words, my heart goes back 30 years, to Pakistan, where Khadar, my highly intelligent bearer, wants passionately to have me buy him a transistor radio from the PX, because the other "boys" own them; his wife is going to have a baby, he has no job lined up, and I am about to leave the country. We are both in tears as I lecture on thrift and prudence—thrift and prudence! hardly the watchwords of my life—and I refuse to buy him the radio. Well, the baby dies anyway, I learn much later when I am safely home. And Janeway has me in tears again, remembering.)

Another insight has to do with "our own general commitment to the need we perceive to keep things running": We have habitually cooked, scrubbed, minded the store and the baby; even if well-off, we have run the errands, made the appointments, picked up the cleaning, driven the children to the dentist and the dancing class, and so on. Well, why not? our men inquire, in reasonable tones. It's not as if these jobs were so arduous, compared to the world's work, which wears them out. Most of our responsibilities don't even require any special talents or training. That, of course, is the point: the trivial nature of the chores of the daily round. "The combination of everydayness with femininity has, in fact, worked to trivialize both. Our commitment to keep things running, without protest as a group, without offering and insisting on new ideas and new ways . . . has operated as a very strong social control on ambition and achievement in other fields." Even as this is being written, more and more couples are concerning themselves with the equitable distribution of trivial tasks. It is fashionable to write about this as if it were a worldwide trend, rather than a series of individual patchwork arrangements. Janeway suggests that we turn our attention to broader political and social solutions, without being terribly specific about them. Who can be? It hasn't been tried before, and we have to work it out as we go along.

Female sexuality, Janeway believes, "has always been used by society as a sort of glue to hold structures together. . . . Attempts are still made to enlist its aid in preserving order within family and social relationships, but more and more they take on the air of desperate bricolage. The power of sexuality is being invoked in semimagical fashion, to support outworn paradigms that no longer explain and predict events in the world. The salt has lost its savor, the glue its glueyness." These paradigms have been imposed from without. "They do not grow out of the interior emotional reality of the female self." And, "coming out of an alien understanding as they do, they are never really satisfactory, even when they seem to be accepted and absorbed quite thoroughly." Masculine visions of female sexuality "are attempts to manipulate woman's vision of herself."

When it was useful for men to see us as ravenous lustful tools of Satan, they did so, egged on by a powerful Church. In Victorian times, however, we suddenly became pale frigid creatures, clamped onto our pedestals by the Protestant church as the exemplars of moral authority. Heigh-ho! No wonder we've had to keep loose and watch the signals. Now the failure of the old paradigms forces us to look for new ones. How? when we have not yet had enough time living "as free people in shared authenticity," to give our minds free play. We can begin, however, to define ourselves by what we do not want. "We do not want to reglue ourselves into a social structure that is essentially patriarchal. We do not want to accept the mothering function as central to our true identity, and we should certainly be wary of the attempts now being made to make us chief, if not sole, child raisers, attempts that in the '50s enjoyed a relative success. . . . The proliferation of novels and films featuring deserted husbands, aghast at having to manage personal lives, stunned with self-pity, has this as an end."

Central to change is to understand where we are. To know this, we must understand where we have been. To know *that*, "we must understand *process* as the first step to managing change." This is what Elizabeth Janeway is all about.

Cross Sections From a Decade of Change, by Elizabeth Janeway. New York, Morrow, 1982.

The Women
We Feared to Become:
Alice Adams

"Megan watches Connie, observing her as closely as she can, without appearing to spy. And she concludes that Connie is a perfectly nice, unattractive, perfectly ordinary woman.

"She is rich, of course, her voice is loud and somewhat rude, in the way of the very rich. But George probably knew a lot of very rich girls. And Megan wonders: Could it have been Connie's very ordinariness that he found so appealing? Are some men put off by extremes of intelligence or even attractiveness in women—put off by superior women? This is a new thought, highly puzzling, unwelcome and difficult to digest. And it is true; she is quite sure of that."

These musings by the chief protagonist of Alice Adams' splendid new novel incorporate not only its title but, not surprisingly, one of its central themes—though the reader should bear in mind that Megan thinks *some* men, not all men, are thus put off. Of the three most interesting men in the book, two of them—Henry Stuyvesant, a poor but well-born kindly leftist intellectual, and Jackson Clay, a gloriously nice and brilliant black trumpet player—are the exceptions who steadfastly prefer superior women. The third, Adam Marr, who becomes a successful playwright, sets up his wife, Janet, in a palatial house in White Plains—not at all the style for these two former Paris expatriates—so that he may abandon her for an exotic model. One of Megan's reactions to this is, well, now Janet can go on to med school. Which Janet does.

The four "superior women" of the title meet as Radcliffe classmates. There is Megan, a scholarship girl from California lastingly embarrassed by her background: her parents' store, "whose humiliating slogan is WE BUY JUNQUE, WE SELL ANTIQUES," and her brassy-haired mother's delight in her new-found career as a carhop. Megan keeps quiet about her origins; she "looks and watches and absorbs." There is Lavinia, from Washington, D.C., beautiful, rich and fashionable; there is Peg, big, clumsy, motherly and even richer; there is Cathy, a rigid Catholic, the least clearly delineated of the four. Janet, the Jew, is a peripheral character, partly owing to Lavinia's snobbish anti-Semitism: "Megan, Megan, you're such a California innocent. If you'd ever lived in a big city where there're lots of them you'd *know*." Megan is upset by this but is unable to counter Lavinia's "flawless sophistication."

Later on, when Megan and Cathy become closer friends (the grouping and regrouping of these four, switching confidantes, alternating intimacies, is one of the musical patterns of the novel), Cathy says, "Did you ever read those really old books about girls' boarding schools? Grace Harlow or someone? There were a lot of them at a resort we used to go to. Anyway, there were always four girls. One beautiful and rich and wicked, and one big and fat and jolly. That's Lavinia and Peg, of course." Cathy goes on: "I'm not too clear about the other two. I think one was poor and virtuous and the other one was very smart, or some combination like that." Megan laughs. "Well, I'm poor and you're virtuous, and God knows both of us are smart, so I guess it'll work out all right?" This conversation is recapitulated at the very end of the book, when Peg and Megan, now nearing 60, have set up a kind of commune or shelter for homeless women, which now rather improbably includes as residents Florence, Megan's ex-car-

14

hop mother; Henry, on weekends; and Jackson, for lengthy visits. Clearly Adams means to emphasize the literary, stylized (even idealized, at least at the end) nature of her book. A minor reason for this may be Adams' desire to keep her work from being read as a *roman à clef*, which it assuredly is not. Forget Mary McCarthy and her "group."

However, for those of us who were Western girls who managed to be accepted at the established Eastern women's colleges, on scholarships or partial scholarships, thrown into a strange milieu with arcane attitudes, with clothes a little wrong and accents that provoked gentle laughter, a good deal of identification with Megan is inevitable.

But Megan is unusual—and stronger than many of us were—in that she never seems seriously to consider marriage, or to give a thought to having children. In that sense she is perhaps the "New Woman" that girls of my generation barely dared to dream of becoming. It occurs to me—though Adams may not have intended it—that the other three women (further to reinforce the stylized quality of the novel) function, in part, as what might be called *anima* figures, in that useful term of Jung's. That is, they represent, in one aspect or another, the women we were afraid of being: Peg, our night terrors of being fat, clumsy, unappealing to men; Cathy, our daily fears of becoming passive victims, used by men; Lavinia, (and this, more subtly, the nervous apprehensions of "superior women") that she may be seduced by the things of this world—affluence, possessions, "gracious living"—into relinquishing the serious goals of life in favor of being kept by men.

We American women, unlike our European sisters, I suspect, have such amorphous identities when we are young! We barely know who we are. There are the defiant campus radicals who don't shave their legs and turn up their noses at convention; there are the immaculate sophisticates in their cashmere sweaters and strands of real pearls. And we who are neither try to be both. But life—as Adams so bravely and

15

wittily demonstrates in this novel—cruelly teaches us to become ourselves. And the radicals and sophisticates, who were neither as indifferent to convention nor as enslaved to it as we believed back then, metamorphose, too. At times, they even exchange roles.

All our lives we have been presented with books that explore the initiation rites that introduce young men to maturity. Now we are hearing the women's side. The strain of nostalgia, even pathos, in Adams' book arises from her sensitive awareness of how grown up we have to be before we grow up.

Superior Women, by Alice Adams. New York, Knopf, 1984.

The Education
of Ilka Weissnix:
Lore Segal

More than 20 years ago Lore Segal published a brilliant novel in the form of a memoir, *Other People's Houses*, which recounts the life of a Viennese refugee child who is boarded in a series of English families for seven years. Eventually her parents managed to leave as well, and are now employed as servants in another series of houses. These members of a comfortable middle-class Jewish family are treated as objects of charity, subject to the whims of various employers and bureaucrats. Lore manages to triumph over these vicissitudes with the help of the sharp analytic eye of a born writer. (One wonders if any of the English families so deftly anatomized in *Other People's Houses* ever read the book and felt any pangs other than the nip of the serpent's tooth. One meanly hopes so.)

The memoir goes on to tell of Lore's three years in the Dominican Republic before she and her mother are finally admitted to the United States in 1951, and they have their own house at last. Ten pages from the end of the book a character called Carter Bayoux is introduced, a member of Lore's class in creative writing at the New School. He is "a middle-age Negro . . . who dominated the class with his powerful presence and silence." He invites Lore to dinner the following

17

week. "We will go to a jazz place and give you an introductory course in Americana," Carter says. "I'm a great teacher." After their date, Lore gives a party where Carter seems "nervous and upset." No explanation. Then Carter simply vanishes from the book after four pages.

But now Carter Bayoux is resurrected as the hero—the wounded, potent, self-destructive hero at bay—of *Her First American.*

Many who read the opening chapters of this book in *The New Yorker* were totally captivated. I can't remember wanting so passionately for a story to go on and on since Rebecca West's *The Fountain Overflows.* After three months in New York, Ilka Weissnix, a 21-year-old Viennese refugee, is taking a trip west to discover the real America. Her train makes a 90-minute stop "in the middle of the New World." She discovers her first American in a bar across from the railroad track.

"He bought her a whiskey and asked her what in the name of the blessed Jehoshaphat she was doing in Cowtown, Nevada.

"'Nevada?' Ilka had said. 'I have believed I am being in Utah, isn't it?'

"'Utah!' The big American turned a sick color. 'Where the hell am I?' he asked the barman.

"'Hagen . . . Nevada.' replied the barman and swiped his dish towel at a glass mug.

"'Aha! So!' Ilka sipped her whiskey and hiding her smiling teeth inside her glass, said, 'I do not believe.'

"'What don't you believe?' asked the American.

"'I do not believe Nevada, Utah, America.' . . . "

"'I'll teach you how to drink, he told Ilka." Ilka says that he is her first real American.

"'Of the second class,' said the big man.

"Ilka shook her head and smiled. 'I am understanding always lesser and lesser.'" He replies, "I'm a wonderful teacher."

Who, after reading this far, would not continue?

The American—Carter Bayoux—is a journalist who knows everyone, a prominent black intellectual, he is a former United Nations official, over the hill and going down fast, but above all, sick or well, a didact.

They meet again in New York when Carter Bayoux takes Ilka to a wedding reception where she discovers that he is famous, popular and a drunk. He liberates a bottle of Chivas Regal from the flustered bartender, and swipes capsules from the office of the doctor who is the father of the bride. They meet the bridegroom, who tells him that it is "all right" that Carter has slept with the bride in California.

"'No it's not, young man!' said Carter Bayoux and brought the bottle down onto the bar so that the glasses jumped. Heads turned. Into the sudden silence Carter Bayoux's high, outraged voice said, 'That's not a thing one man says to another! Have you no sense of protocol?'" Protocol.

Carter and Ilka leave and go for coffee, and Carter pops more of the doctor's pills.

"'But about the bridegroom,' said Ilka. 'Protocol does not have to do with human feeling.'

"'Damn tootin',' Carter Bayoux said.

"'I think,' said Ilka, 'the bridegroom meant it friendly. I think he said it humanly, no? He was meaning 'You and I loved the same woman. We have this together.'

"'Oh?' said Carter. 'Is that what he was meaning? I will tell you what the bridegroom was saying. He was saying "I am a white liberal and you're a black son of a bitch.'

He is definitely Negro, thought Ilka with relief.

At dawn the next day, Ilka receives a telegram:

"PROTOCOL IS THE ART OF NOT REPEAT NOT LIVING BY NATURAL HUMAN FEELING STOP BUMP INTO A LONDONER AND HE BEGS YOUR PARDON SO YOU BEG HIS PARDON STOP LONDON RUNS ON PROTOCOL BUT A NEW YORKER BUMPS INTO YOU AND KNOCKS YOU DOWN AND TELLS YOU TO WATCH WHERE YOURE GOING SO YOU KNOCK HIM DOWN AND HE KILLS YOU AND YOU

KILL HIM BACK STOP NEW YORK RUNS ON NATURAL
HUMAN FEELING STOP"

And so their affair begins. Seldom has a more checkered relationship been recorded: preceptor and neophyte, drunk and sobersides, black and white, man of protocol, woman of feeling. Although there are many cunningly woven minor themes, the main lines of the novel have been laid out. Now they dance the variations: dark, hilarious, plangent, full of tears.

One regrets that Carter Bayoux is so far gone when Ilka meets him, groans audibly when Carter plunges yet again into the cycle of drunkenness, compulsive phoning to friends and relatives who gradually give up on him, mental illness followed by periods of grim sobriety. Oh to have known this charmer in his prime! But we, like Ilka, are subject to Ms. Segal's relentless agenda .

For relief, there is a pastoral interlude called "Summer," when Carter is on the wagon, and a large cast of characters, black and white, assemble in a rambling house in Connecticut. Their interactions provide us with a lavish display of Ms. Segal's virtuosity and wit; you read it smiling all the time.

And there are some marvelous set pieces: one a meeting of Alcoholics Anonymous, a prime exhibit of Ms. Segal's faultless ear for dialogue, with hair-raising authenticity. Another is Carter's interview with Ulalia, a gospel singer, when in response to Carter's statement "I'm talking about what I have called the fear-hate-fear complex which inevitably, I believe, afflicts the Negro in a racist society," the singer replies, "Fear God, keep His commandments; for this is the whole duty of man." Ecclesiastes twelve, thirteen.

In the epigraph to *Other People's Houses*, Ms. Segal says: "The 'Carter Bayoux' of my book once told me a story out of his childhood. When he had finished, I said that I knew just where his autobiography had stopped and fiction began. He said, 'Then you know more than I.'"

Though *Her First American* does not have epic sweep and

20

and physical bulk, though it was not written by a man, though its main characters are a number of black Americans and a handful of Jewish refugees in New York City—admittedly not "the real America"—Lore Segal may have come closer than anyone to writing The Great American Novel. Essentially, this novel is about how we behave to one another, and the consequences of that behavior. It's about how we lose by winning, how we are educated by loving, how we change and are changed by everyone we know. Ms. Segal, in her mix of history, memory and invention, and the ruthless honesty which has always characterized her work, shows us ourselves, and reveals herself: Hitler's gift to us, a real American.

Her First American, by Lore Segal. New York, Knopf, 1985.

Section II

WOMEN
AFRAID

Two Women Terrified:
Eleanor Clark

S ome of my friends and I first came to Eleanor Clark's *Rome and a Villa* because our mothers pressed it on us with eager hands. Those aging sedentary housewives who had traveled largely in their imagination took vicarious joy in its opulence of experience and learning. For once we listened to them, and read a book they loved. Having begun, who could resist it? We too were enamored of its style and its stylishness, and have cherished Miss Clark ever since for the immaculate writer and intuitive witness that she is.

Witnessing: woman's role and art. What would we—all of us—lose if women succeeded in entering the arena as the equals of men, at the expense of that witnessing? From Jane Austen and Emily Brontë to Emily Dickinson and Marianne Moore, the view from the sidelines has produced a precious hoard. But Eleanor Clark is still witnessing, and recording the decline and fall of the West with a heated energy beyond despair.

Her novel, *Camping Out*, continues to develop the themes that have obsessed her for so long. There are antecedents in her earlier novel, *Gloria Mundi*, a horrified elegy for the state of Vermont and its death by snowmobile, by cabin cruiser, by truckers with CBs, by drifters and weekend hunters, bulldozers and motorcycle gangs, by oafish tourists, hotshot real-estate agents and environmental rapists, hippie entrepreneurs and drug-dazed offspring of the summer people—reminding one of those noble and neglected poems of Hayden Carruth on the same subject.

Evil surrounds us, not only in these visible, palpable forms, but in the fears it creates: of the sullen alien waiting to board the plane; the shadow of a stranger cast across the picnic table; nocturnal sounds—a rustle, a squeak, a whisper—that seem to signal a malign presence lurking nearby.

In *Camping Out*, Dennie, the decorous wife of a foreign service officer in Rome, has returned to New England for the funeral of her mother. A friend whom she had known casually in Rome, a lesbian poet named Marilyn, shows up and persuades her to come on an ill-advised camping trip to a remote lake in Vermont. It goes without saying that the worst, short of actual murder, happens.

For once, one doesn't hesitate to reveal something of the plot because Ms. Clark deliberately telegraphs her punches, like a 12th century Chinese poet who tells you in each verse what she plans for the next one. As the canny author knows, if anything this adds to the suspense. Another daring strategy is the breaking off into soliloquies by Dennie as violent events are about to take place virtually under her nose, a device more familiar in recollection of things past than in happenstance. This frequently seems strained, and one cannot help speculating that, given Ms. Clark's own loss of eyesight, a focus on the present can hardly be borne, and must be continually shifted to the remembered past.

The threat who predictably appears is named Fred, or perhaps Isaac, or Luigi, or Denton or Gerhardt. A drifter, perhaps an escapee from a nearby prison, a boaster of the multiple murders that in all probability he has committed, Fred shows up just after the two naked women have been making love on the beach, to announce that he has witnessed it all. He is clearly dangerous, sinister, even diabolic (he smells of sulfur); he slices a hole in the women's canoe and steals their paddle upon leaving, and it is all too clear that he will return.

Why the women don't take to their heels at this point is one of the puzzles and irritations of this novel. To say that otherwise there wouldn't be a novel isn't good enough; but Fred exerts some peculiar fascination on Dennie and Marilyn. I'm afraid that it has something to do with the fact that he lapses from street talk into educated English from time to time, and he plays Mozart with great skill on a penny whistle.

One finds the genesis of Fred and his terror of their little dog (which the women, inexplicably, tie up when he asks them to) in Miss Clark's poignant memoir about losing her vision in *Eyes, Etc.*: Eleanor and a young girl, on an overnight camping trip, are alone when their men are off exploring or fishing. A sinister stranger looms up, becomes livid at the antics of their little English cocker spaniel, and threatens to kill it if it comes a step closer. "He was nursing some terrible, probably congenital rage and consumed with hunger for something to take it out on." Eleanor halloos for the men across the lake, and they return in a hurry. This "irate man, trembler before small dogs, hater of all fellow men," becomes, eight years later, the awful Fred, who kills the little dog and has two frightened and hypnotized women at his mercy, with no rescuing men on the other side of the lake.

Another narrative, clearly of deep significance to Miss Clark, occurs first in the new edition of *Rome and a Villa*. My mother's copy was lost on an unreturned loan (to someone who couldn't bear to give it up, I expect). So, tempted by an added chapter about the Protestant Cemetery, I bought this volume with its new introduction, "Return to Rome." Here is an account of Assunta, "that grand plebeian character," a gifted dressmaker living in an enormous ruined fortress during World War II, with her destitute family. The landlady for these and other fugitives from the bombed-out villages below is a rich miserly spinster referred to as "the Signorina of the Rocca." This lady had conceived a passion for her confessor, and in one mad burst of extravagance had acquired the fortress at the behest of "this rake of a Monsignore."

Episodes: A downed American pilot is torn to pieces in the street in nearby Orbetello. The remains of another American airman are found wedged in the rocks below the fortress. Assunta's husband, Giuseppe, comes back from a prisoner-of-war camp, as weak and wayward as ever. Now, in *Camping Out*, the story recurs, this time as a tale within a tale, spoken by Dennie into Marilyn's tape recorder as they sit around the fire in camp.

Very little has changed: Assunta is Assunta. Giuseppe has become Ottavio, with the same character, or lack of it. Dennie herself is a child living in the Rocca with her mother and twin brother. It is the spring of 1948; her parents are separated. The forced-down flyer has been torn to pieces by the villagers, who had been bombed by mistake. Under the water, midnight-blue at the lighthouse point, an American pilot's body had been found the year before. A bunch of young Black Shirts use Dennie's Raggedy Ann doll for target practice.

These and other reminiscences of Dennie serve to delay the long-anticipated violence, but finally what we know will happen happens. A great many women will be affronted by the rape scene, because Marilyn has repeated orgasms while being raped. Back we go, to that ancient, smirking male cliché: "They really want it!" And the rage of lesbian readers can all too readily be imagined. Furthermore, Dennie, listening outside the tent where, between the cries of orgasm, dulcet conversations are going on, fancies herself jealous, regrets that Fred didn't choose her! Even more bewildering is the scene when the women, after a harrowing escape from Fred, moving cross-country during a ferocious storm, finally encounter a deputy sheriff. Not a word do they mention of Fred, the multiple murderer, on the loose somewhere around the lake. Instead, they take pains to cover up for him.

At the very end of the book, Miss Clark piles on new revelations involving incest, an improbable adultery, and the reappearance of their old antagonist, Fred, laughing on an Italian beach. It's all gratuitous, and amazing. But over all, the

amazement one feels is at the astonishing *energy* of the book—
as if Eleanor Clark, in her 70's, had summoned all her consid-
erable powers to emit one pure Maenad shriek of fury at the
masters of civilization and their degenerate get, who foul our
world. Fred is their product, and her characters forgive him.
Her readers will not find it so easy.

Camping Out, by Eleanor Clark. New York, Putnam, 1986.

Mrs. Lessing's Nightmare:
Doris Lessing

Ms. Lessing's novel, *The Fifth Child*, is a moral fable, of the *genre* which includes Mary Shelley's *Frankenstein* and George Orwell's *1984*. The introduction to the Everyman edition of *Frankenstein* defines it thus: "The theme has all the power and freshness of a myth: that is to say, it articulates . . . a deeply felt cultural neurosis." All three of these works derive their energy in part from their echoes of ancient epics and "Titanic" heroes (who function as effectively when hero becomes heroine).

Because all three authors have read widely, there are literary echoes as well: *Paradise Lost* especially, a tinge of Faustian *hubris*, which emphasize, without moralizing, the novel as cautionary tale. Ms. Shelley's cultural neuroses and personal traumas are buried deep, deep within her story (a story, after all, written by a girl still in her teens). For Orwell, the culture *is* the story.

With her *Canopus* series of novels, Ms. Lessing seemed, in despair, to turn her back on our culture and fly to outer space. Now, to the relief of many of her long-time admirers, she has returned to earth, to deal in her customary forthright fashion with our flawed and crumbling social fabric.

In *1984*, Orwell, speaking through the voice of Emmanuel Goldstein, says that, "the economy of many countries was allowed to stagnate, land went out of cultivation, capital equipment was not added to, great blocks of the population were prevented from working and kept half alive by State charity." Margaret Drabble's fine novel, *The Radiant Way*, explored the changing lives of three Englishwomen in the physically and morally deteriorating environment of London today. Now Ms. Lessing combines what Ellen Moers called Mary Shelley's "waking dream of monster-manufacture" with Orwell's prediction of social decay. The monster-child born to the nice, normal Lovatt couple eventually finds his true home in the monster-company of the underclass: the uneducable, the unemployable, the rootless, whose vacuity leads them inevitably to drugs, violence and crime.

The Fifth Child begins when Harriet and David meet at an office party in the late 1960s. They seem like freaks to their friends and associates because they epitomize the traditional values of family and fidelity so violently overthrown in the upheavals of those times. Harriet is a virgin, although she prefers to think of herself as "something like a present wrapped in layers of deliciously pretty paper, to be given, with discretion, to the right person. Her own sisters laughed at her." As her grandmother's generation might have said, "She's no better than she ought to be." Her contemporaries say to each other, "It must be something in her childhood that's made her like this. Poor thing."

David has had one disastrous affair with a girl who was his utter opposite. He believes that since they broke up, she has slept with everyone in his office. She too is at the party, blowing him frantic kisses, but he is making his way, across a crowded room, towards the thoughtful, quiet figure of Harriet in an unfashionable blue dress.

When they retreat to an empty office to talk, they discover that their ideals and goals are nearly identical although their backgrounds are quite different. Harriet comes from a stable home with contented parents. David's parents divorced when he was small. Now David knew the kind of woman he wanted and needed. "His wife must be like him in this: that she knew where happiness lay and how to keep it."

Very soon they marry. Why wait? They find a large Victorian house a long commute from London, a house they can't afford, with plenty of space for children and guests. But they meant to have a lot of both. Harriet, who had planned on working for a year or two to help finance the house purchase, becomes pregnant almost immediately. Their first child, Luke, was an easy child, so they go ahead with plans for a large family gathering at Easter, the first of many parties for their extended family and friends. For the next few years the birth of three more children hardly puts a damper on the continuing festivities. Even when she is exhausted, Harriet has a compulsive need to keep open house as a validation of the life that she and David have chosen. "Listening to the laughter, the voices, the talk, the sounds of children playing, Harriet and David . . . would reach for each other's hand and smile, and breathe happiness." There is a disturbing hint of *hubris* in their self-satisfaction. When Harriet's unhappily married sister gives birth to a mongol child, Harriet doesn't believe that it is a case of bad luck. No, their misery, their quarrels have brought this mongol child upon them.

Meanwhile, the economic situation deteriorates; David barely manages to hang on to his job; their safe little town has become another magnet for brutal crimes. "There was an ugly edge on events: more and more it seemed that two peoples lived in England, not one—enemies, hating each other, who could not hear what the other said." Or, as Orwell's Goldstein puts it, "There was a vast amount of criminality in London, a whole world-within-a-world of thieves, bandits, prostitutes, drug peddlers and racketeers of every description, but since it all happened among the proles themselves, it was of no importance."

Although Harriet has never had an easy time with her pregnancies, this fifth one is different, frighteningly so. The energy of the fetus, beating a tattoo on her belly, keeps her from rest or sleep. "Phantoms and chimeras inhabited her brain. She would think, When the scientists make experiments, welding two kinds of animal together, of different sizes, then I suppose this is what the poor mother feels. She imagined pathetic botched creatures horribly real to her . . . " This will remind readers of Shelley's book, or those who remember one of the many film versions, of Frankenstein's horror at the poor, botched thing he has patched together from diverse pieces, not the radiant being of his imagination.

When at last Ben is born, he doesn't look like a normal baby but like some troll or goblin. Harriet finds herself thinking, "I wonder what the mother would look like, the one who would welcome this alien." At various times, Ms. Lessing describes Ben as a Neanderthal, a dwarf, a being forging metal deep under the earth with his kind, as well as intimating that he is a creature from another planet.

Before he is six months old, Ben has begun to destroy their family life. He has grasped his little brother Paul's arm through the bars of his crib and badly sprained it. No one needs to tell the other children to be careful. One of their few remaining guests brings along a little terrier. Ben strangles it, and later murders the old family cat. Now, in the mid-'seventies, most of their former guests make excuses for not coming to visit. The world that David and Harriet constructed for themselves has fallen apart. Paradise lost indeed.

Finally, before he is three, Ben begins to talk. His first words are, "I want." "I want cake." "Give me that." "His voice was heavy and uncertain, each word separate, as if his brain were a lumber-house of ideas and objects, and he had to identify each one." (Frankenstein's monster says, "I learned and applied the words, *fire, milk, bread* and *wood*.") Watching over Ben, trying to teach him something resembling normal behavior, absorbs all of Harriet's time and energy, to the neglect of her four charming older children.

Still, out of anger and guilt, Harriet strives to be a proper mother to Ben, as if, though he cannot express himself in such a phrase, he were saying what Frankenstein's monster said to

33

him: "Remember, I am thy creature . . . "

Keeping their efforts a secret from Harriet, other members of the family arrange for Ben to be institutionalized. When Ben goes, the other children are filled with hysterical relief. In the days that follow, "the family expanded like paper flowers in water." But Harriet is hounded by Ben's fate, and forces her mother-in-law to divulge the name of the place where Ben is incarcerated.

There follows an almost unbearably dramatic and harrowing scene. After a long drive north, Harriet forces her way in, traversing a long ward crowded with Nature's mistakes: "A baby like a comma, great lolling head on a stalk of a body . . . then something like a stick insect, enormous bulging eyes among still fragilities that were limbs . . . A child seemed at first glance normal, but then Harriet saw there was no back to its head; it was all face, which seemed to scream at her . . . "

Then she reaches Ben, naked inside a strait-jacket in an isolation room smeared with urine and excrement. "I told you not to come!" screams the young attendant. They pluck up Ben and hose him down; tranquilized and wrapped in blankets, he is thrown in the back of Harriet's car and she drives him home in the wintry rain. She is met with the open hostility of her husband and children. "They felt that she had turned her back on them and chosen to go off into an alien country, with Ben."

Harriet finds John, an unemployed layabout, and bribes him to look after Ben during the day. Ben rides off on the back of John's motorcycle, to become a kind of mascot for John's gang. Usually he is away till long after suppertime. But his siblings lock their doors at night. And the year when Ben turns five, the older children choose to go to boarding school, against their parents' egalitarian principles. This happens shortly after they all come down to breakfast and find Ben squatting on the table tearing a raw chicken apart with his teeth and hands.

"Poor Ben hungry," he whines. He has taken to calling himself Poor Ben.

Eventually all the "real children" drift away, to live with

grandparents or collateral relatives, or in the case of Paul, the youngest, a once high-spirited and friendly child now a bundle of nerves and rage, to stay with his psychiatrist. David, partly to help pay for schools and therapy, works longer and longer hours, and is home less and less. Harriet is alone in the huge house with Ben and his layabout pals.

In time, John moves on, but soon Ben attracts a crowd of friends: "the uneducable, the unassimilable, the hopeless, who move up the school from class to class, waiting for the happy moment when they can leave." Harriet can't believe that Ben can be accepted by any group. But to her astonishment, she finds that he is a leader. They become Ben's gang, Billy, Vic, Elvis and the rest, all television junkies lapping up the shootings and killings and torture and fightings.

Ben is away for longer and longer intervals as Harriet reads in the papers of mugging, hold-ups, break-ins. The outcome is clear: Ben and his friends will drift off to the city and vanish into its nether world, living in its derelict buildings, finding their thrills in street fights and riots, to end up in prison or the morgue.

In Goldstein's voice, Orwell says that, "as a whole, the world is more primitive today than it was fifty years ago." When the real 1984 came around, in a flurry of self-congratulation we assured ourselves that Orwell's bleak prognostications had not come to pass. A scant ten years later, we may take a less sanguine view. The distance between the Lovatts and their friends and the Bens and their friends becomes more of a chasm with each passing season. The decent liberals among us still hang on to the hope that, with massive infusions of money, we can repair the infrastructure, educate, train and house the ignorant, the unskilled, the homeless. I don't believe that Ms. Lessing is among them, absorbed as she is in Orwell's night-mare of social collapse and Mary Shelley's "horror story of Maternity." Doris Lessing is a better writer than poor Mary, and writes as well as Orwell, than which there is no higher praise.

The Fifth Child, by Doris Lessing. New York, Knopf, 1988.

Section III

ODD WOMEN

A Power in the House:
Ivy Compton-Burnett

We who are devotees of the novels of Ivy Compton-Burnett (the latter half of her name pronounced "burn it!") picture her always as an old lady—as indeed she was in the 'forties, when Americans began to read her—a prim, didactic, judgmental old character whose hairstyle remained unchanged from the 1920s until she died in her eighties. Her dialogue—and her novels consist largely of dialogue, mordant and stylized—is reminiscent of none other than Jane Austen, if one can picture Austen as old, tough, hard-bitten, iconoclastic and utterly without illusions. But there the similarity ends. Austen's chief topic was marriage and how to achieve it. Compton-Burnett's topic is power, the power that tyrannical parents (or aunts, or uncles, or butlers) exert over the helpless. Although all her finest novels are set around the turn of the century, it is not difficult to extrapolate from these accounts of domestic tyranny the world as portrayed by Orwell or Kafka, or even such works as William Shirer's *The Rise and Fall of the Third Reich*.

The novels, which customarily begin at the breakfast table, never stray from hearth and home. If a character takes a trip, he or she disappears from the text. Compton-Burnett's basilisk eye is fixed on the interplay between tyrant and victim and their collaboration in their respective roles. There are always witnesses—children, governesses, servants, eld-

erly aunts—to comment on the action in muffled or whis-
pered voices, as the author herself never does. It is clear that
the lady was mistress of all the permutations of power and its
corruptions. How did she acquire this knowledge? That is the
subject—and the fascination—of this full and frank biography.

Ivy Compton-Burnett was the oldest child of her father's
second family. His first marriage produced six children, the
last of whom survived his mother at his birth. Exactly one
year later, Dr. Burnett (the compound and hyphen were
added later by his second wife) remarried, and Ivy was born
nine months after that, to be followed in quick succession by
six siblings. Of these 12 children (a son by the first wife died at
age 2) only one of them married. Of that large Victorian
family, many of them brilliant and attractive, there came no
other marriages, and no descendants. This reluctance to per-
petuate the line would seem to speak for itself.

Was Dr. Burnett, then, the tyrant who served as Ivy's
model? No; by all accounts he was a kind man, although he
spent little time at home with his family, commuting to their
house in the country from his (homeopathic) practice in
Harley Street, London. (Dr. Burnett's views on women would
hardly appeal to feminists, past or present, as he held to a
theory that, every month "the damsel throws away" what he
named "pelvic power"; so, from the onset of menarche, life is
all downhill for women.)

Was the second wife a monster mother? It seems not,
although after Dr. Burnett's death in 1901, she gave way to
such hysterical and prolonged grief that the burden on her
family, particularly her eldest son, Guy, was nearly insup-
portable. His death of pneumonia four years later, when he
was 20, was probably inevitable, given his state of exhaustion
and depression.

Who, then, was the archetypal villain or villainess from
whom Ivy learned so much? Why, it seems that it was Ivy
herself! "Well, a house must have a head," as one of her
characters remarks.

40

When her mother died in 1911, Ivy moved smartly into her place. By the terms of her mother's will, Ivy and her remaining brother Noel became guardians to their four little sisters until they were 24 (which meant another 12 years in captivity for the youngest). Ivy was 27, Noel 24. She took over the business affairs of the family and managed the money until the trust fund was wound up, 50 years later. "To the schoolroom party it seemed as though nothing had changed . . . she oversaw their investments, arranged their education, interviewed their teachers, dealt out their allowances and generally assumed power over her sisters."

Ivy's bossiness became intolerable for the four little girls; all of them were markedly musical and were to study with famed pianist Myra Hess, who was then living nearby. However, Ivy was dead to music. She forbade piano playing under her roof and the little girls were forced to have their mother's Bechstein carried to a hired music room around the corner. "We didn't develop as she had chosen; she became very critical," one of the sisters said later. To which Spurling adds, "Her rule was quiet, orderly and cruel. Power seems to have been to her less an emotional gratification than a tactical advantage which she could no more help exploiting than her sisters could help but concede."

Her brother Noel, who had taken Guy's place in Ivy's affections, went off, following a brilliant career at Cambridge and a pitifully brief (and probably unconsummated) marriage, to the trenches of World War I and was killed in 1916, in one of the senseless battles of that senseless war.

At the time of Noel's marriage, the younger girls had summoned the courage to rebel. They took their own house in London and shared it with Myra Hess, where they thought they might "get on quite well" on their combined allowances, eked out by the sale of their mother's jewelry. They drew lots to see who should break the news to Ivy. In October 1915, as Noel marched towards the Western Front, the family house was sold, its possessions divided among the children, and the

41

faithful housekeeper Minnie—prototype of so many substitute mothers in Ivy's fiction—accompanied the younger girls to their new home in St. John's Wood. Ivy had no home, nothing to do, and nowhere to go. She suggested to her sisters that she move in with them. They politely and firmly declined.

But even this bitterly won freedom was evidently not enough to save the two youngest sisters. It came too late, after too many deaths and too many power struggles. Topsy, 22, and Primrose, 18, locked themselves in their bedroom, took Veronal and died in each other's arms, in December 1917.

Ivy felt that her life was over. And indeed, *that* life was. Beginning in 1925 (discounting a piece of juvenilia called *Dolores*, written 14 years earlier, which Ivy dismissed from her canon), Ivy began to write, without faltering, in the full maturity of her style, the nineteen novels that made her fame. She is exceptional, if not unique, in founding her novels on her own period of tyranny, in the years when, as her sister Vera said, "Ivy wasn't master of herself—something was mastering her, and it wasn't the best part of her." An extraordinary detachment, a breathtaking self-knowledge!

In October 1919, the pattern of Ivy's new life was set. Margaret Jourdain, a sometime poet and a renowned authority on furniture—with a galaxy of friends, mostly gay and hugely entertaining—moved into Ivy's flat, which they shared for the next thirty-one years. In this amusing, witty, gossipy society, Ivy for the first time in her life took a back seat. She was the quiet companion of an eminent woman. She said little and poured the tea. Then her novels began to appear at regular intervals, to remarkable critical acclaim but small popular success. Eventually, Margaret's friends began to pay attention to Ivy, at which Margaret's pleasure was not unalloyed.

Margaret was eight years Ivy's senior; when she died, Ivy was devastated. She never really recovered. Nevertheless, she gradually added literary friends to the faithful members of Margaret's circle, and there was a kind of late blooming that lasted until Ivy's death at eighty-six.

Spurling's biography does her justice and must increase her readership. However, I would wish that, long as this biography is, it told us more of the last years of the four younger sisters and of Dame Myra Hess. Perhaps some-day . . . .

Ivy: The Life of Ivy Compton-Burnett, by Hilary Spurling. New York, Knopf, 1984.

Becoming Renata Adler:
Carolyn Kizer

"Do you suppose," said my friend, the cleverest critic in the Western World, "they send us these books for review because we live way out here, and they can feel reasonably sure that we aren't pals of the author?"

"It's possible," I sighed. "It certainly seems as if she writes the inside of the book for her friends, and her friends write the outside of the book for her."

"Yes, it's a bit much when the back flap quotes a woman— a nice, sensible woman too—as saying that *Speedboat* is an occasion for pride and hope for the human race."

"I once blurbed that somebody was Mozartean, and I've been kicking myself ever since."

"Are you trying to tell me that you judged that book by its cover?" the C.C. inquired, a bit acerbically.

"I didn't when I just re-read it. Slight, but nicely written, I'd say. One can forgive the obligatory reference to Elaine's, the party celebrity lists, even her curious obsession—which crops up again in *Pitch Dark*—with John O'Hara. John O'Hara who, she says, taught her generation of girls about love. You're about her age. What about that?"

"Why not Spike Jones?"

I refilled the coffee cups. "In a sense, we all write for our friends, living and dead—a bunch of Antonia Krögers. But shouldn't we cast our nets widely?—like a friendly Whitman rather than the type who drew a circle and shut us out?"

"One does feel like the Reader Over Her Shoulder."

"It's more like the Eavesdropper on the Party Line. Except of course we were meant to overhear."

"And eat our hearts out?"

*   *   *   *   *

When Bill phoned, I said, "'Flu. I can't possibly make it to Chez Panisse tonight." Chez Panisse is nicer than Elaine's. For one thing, it's handy, right at the foot of the hill. For another, Alice Waters' cuisine is to Elaine's what Air France food is to any American carrier. Our recent Nobelist likes to hang out in her café.

Oh heck, I have to go back and re-write the above: When Bill, the distinguished memoirist and poet, whom I happen to know very well, phoned . . .

"Anyhow, I'm feeling much too irritable—partly the 'flu, and having to finish this miserable review—if indeed the latter isn't contributing to the former."

"How do you mean?"

"Well, something has happened to the way she writes. Take this passage: 'Clamped to the foot of the Arabian horse of thought, report or feeling, there were always the teeth of the question: is this altogether true?'"

"It makes my fillings ache," Bill said.

"Also, Adler keeps repeating the phrase, 'What do you tell the Sanger people, Lily asked.' Four times in four pages. It turns out Lily's trying to find out about birth control. Pity Adler didn't read more Mary McCarthy and less John O'Hara."

"So it goes," Bill said, and went off mournfully to dine alone.

However, there's a nice bit that comes along later; I went on speaking to Bill as though he were still on the phone. "Sometimes he loved her, sometimes he was just amused and touched by the degree to which she loved him. Sometimes he was bored by her love and felt it as a burden. Sometimes his

45

sense of himself was enhanced, sometimes diminished by it. But he had come to take the extent of her love as given, and as such, he lost interest in it." We can all relate to that.

*   *   *   *   *

Marianna dropped by to return my tape-recorder. She was one of those people one knew in school, who married a would-be poet named Arthur Fish, with a high forehead and thinning red hair. His propensity for streaking through Magnin's lingerie department mattered bitterly to her, and she broke it off.

"You're busy. I won't stay," Marianna cried, retreating from my sneezes.

"But there are a couple of good and interesting set pieces in this book," I said. "One of them about a dying raccoon who comes to sit on her stove; it stays in the mind, even one fogged with 'flu. But then she has to go and say—after an old man and a boy from the Wildlife Commission come and take the raccoon away, perfectly polite and innocent-seeming folks—'God knows what they did with him. Stoned him, probably.'"

Yes, yes, it's no doubt symbolic of the increasing paranoia of our time, blah, blah, blah—but nevertheless it spoils one of the few warmly observed scenes in the book. And it's too bad she pats herself on the back for it later: "He took the story. Some time later, the phone rang. It wasn't you. It rang again: it was you saying, 'I haven't finished, but, Kate, the raccoon.'"

*   *   *   *   *

"In *Pitch Dark*, she's ever more prone to rather elaborate introductions of characters who then sink without a trace."

"As in life," you say.

"But Charlotte, surely you're not trying to maintain that art should be like life?"

"Her friends will write unpleasant letters to the paper."

"The paper likes that." I could have been worse. I might have compared our heroine to William Buckley: these people who have so much, yet still are impelled to boast.

46

"One of the things that bugs me," I say to you who have just flown home on the Red Eye from New York, and don't really need this conversation, "is a passage like the following: 'And though I know my heart cannot have been broken in these things, these things of my house and of yours, no, it can't have been, I'm sure it was not, I find that I am crying as I write, because, it cannot either, can't it? have cost so much to say in some of these things, in some others sometime, not grudgingly, and without reluctance, yes.'"

"It doesn't help when you read it like Siobhan McKenna doing a Chinese accent," he said. I mean, *you* say. "There are lots of passages in Faulkner that would sound just as terrible."

"But why would anyone want to write bad Faulkner, with a dash of Hemingway, James and Stein thrown in, when she can write so well and simply about the raccoon? And there's another fine set piece about Ireland, where her paranoia—if you've ever lived in Ireland—seems perfectly appropriate, and very funny as well. Although in part of it she keeps repeating a line about driving down a road and turning around, very much like the Sanger number, till you want to scream, 'All *right*, already!'"

Beethoven's Wind Octet was on the stereo. "Darling, please stop it before it gets to the bit that sounds like Mary had a little lamb."

"It's 'Good Night Ladies,'" you reply.

"Same thing. Look, would you mind reading what I've written so far?" He took the pages. Later, *you* said, "But you haven't told us what the book is *about*."

"It's about the author."

"But it's called a novel."

"Yes. And this is called a review."

Pitch Dark, by Renata Adler. New York, Knopf, 1983.

47

The Wicked Witch of the East: Madame Mao

China's Cultural Revolution was a gigantic human catastrophe on the scale of the Holocaust and Stalin's Great Terror, blackening not only the twentieth century but the whole of our species. Those who regard it as of lesser magnitude do so only through lack of information. To take up Ross Terrill's book to gain deeper understanding of this decade of horror and folly is to be grievously disappointed.

Terrill, hitherto a respected reporter on Asian affairs, has cobbled together a compendium of personal gossip and highly colored episodes based on dubious sources. Other than material gained from personal interviews, Terrill depends on stories gleaned from organs of Chinese propaganda, including newspapers like *The People's Daily,* and reports from Taiwan, the Soviet Union, and the U.S. consulate general in Hong Kong, each with its own axe to grind.

Despite the bias of his sources, Terrill can't help admiring his leading lady for her guts in standing up to her interrogators at the trial of the Gang of Four, as her co-defendants trembled, confessed, and collapsed. He gives short shrift to these other crucial figures, as well as largely ignoring the social and historical causes of the Cultural Revolution which gained momentum and gradually spun out of control, involving millions of people, most of whom must have had almost as poor an idea of what was going on as we do. In fact, Terrill's book might well have been titled "The Gang of One."

Even readers who depend on *People* magazine for the type of information they are interested in should beware. Mme. Mao, as is well known, once played Nora in *A Doll's House* in Shanghai, during her relatively brief career as a second-rate actress. Terrill makes no less than fifteen comparisons of Mme. Mao with poor little Nora—as if her infamous career could be explained in part by her desire to break out of a conventional bourgeois marriage! He also compares this Messalina with Eleanor Roosevelt (six times), Nancy Reagan and Rosalynn Carter (twice each), and—of all people—Gertrude Stein! "For the moment she was a person in a vacuum, a thoroughbred in search of her species, a Gertrude Stein of the netherworld to which Chinese culture and Communist politics consigned such a woman." Lord have mercy.

The previous quotation is not an isolated example of writing run wild. Consider the following: "Her appearance could change strikingly from one day to the next, as her emotions made a plaything of her body, and illness began its lifelong *pas de deux* with her moods." "Shanghai was a cauldron of contradictions, a city that wore its heart on its sleeve and took in its stride the epoch's kaleidoscope of greed, thrills and death." "Her approach was to . . . permit an occasional, sudden shaft of flirtatiousness to play on the soft underbelly of his personality." The kaleidoscope of moods in my soft underbelly is, in a word, nausea.

Meanwhile, in this welter of rich, hideous prose, the ordeal of millions—murdered, tortured, publicly humiliated to the point where many committed suicide, or were said to have—intellectuals and their children exiled to remote agricultural districts to do manual labor in the fields for as much as a decade—all this goes unmentioned by our reporter. Oh, there is an occasional account of the mistreatment of a high official, or someone who had offended Mme. Mao in the past—this too based on sources hardly better than gossip. But nothing is said about the raids on private homes, the destruc-

49

tion of libraries, the desecration of the tombs of the great poets, China's great and ancient culture gone underground when not wiped out. One of the mightiest sagas of human infamy is reduced to accounts of the spiteful actions of one ambitious female. Our former First Ladies, though an ambitious lot on the whole, cannot by any stretch of the imagination be compared with this creature. However, there is a contemporary figure who, given the ultimate power that he clearly craved, might be given a glancing comparison, and that is Richard Nixon.

There is a nice photograph of Mr. Nixon and Mme. Mao in this book, at a performance of her pet production, *The Red Detachment of Women,* in 1972. There, side by side, are the companionable grins of a pair of pussycats gorged on canary meat. Nixon, too, remained defiant, never expressed regret for his actions. Some people admire him for this.

There are also certain resemblances between Mme. Mao and Ronald Reagan, though Terrill doesn't point to them. He refers to "the thinness of her knowledge and her staggering subjectivity," illustrated by this episode: "Talking of the Indo-China border war, she found its essence in the story of one Indian soldier. He carried his life's savings with him in battle, lost them, and sat down in the Himalayas and cried. A Chinese soldier found the purse of money and managed to have it returned to the Indian soldier, who was overjoyed. The Chinese side was generous, able to be so because of the justice of its cause." Doesn't that way of interpreting current events have a familiar ring?

At present Mme. Mao, sentenced to "manual labor," sits in her cell making cloth dolls, one doll every three days. Recently she has taken to embroidering her name on them, so they are no longer sold but pile up in a warehouse. Some enterprising "capitalist raider" ought to make a deal with the Chinese to export them to us. Wouldn't the cachet of Cabbage Patch dolls fade away, given the chance to purchase your very own Mme. Mao dolly, with her guaranteed personal auto-graph?

A final word: The catastrophic muddle of our policy in Asia for the past 30 years can be attributed in no small part to the decimation of experts who had first-hand knowledge of that area by Senator Joseph McCarthy and the House Un-American Activities Committee. We are still in desperate need of accurate assessments by a new generation of scholars and correspondents. Terrill is of their number. One would like to sentence him to a solitary sabbatical, wherein he would immerse himself in the works of Gibbon, Huizinga and Orwell—Orwell for honor, Orwell for simplicity, Orwell above all for the seeming lack of style which is great style. Please go straight, Mr. Terrill. You are needed.

The White-Boned Demon: A Biography of Madame Mao Zedong, by Ross Terrill. New York, Morrow, 1984.

Section IV

Parents
and
Children

Reading to Children:
'Grill Me Some Bones!'
and Other Delights

When it comes to entertaining children—your own or borrowed ones—the most rewarding activity is reading aloud to them. Almost all children prefer being read to, even unskillfully, to watching any television program, no matter how violent and flashy. We're talking post-Mother Goose and "I'm a Little Teapot" up through grade school here, and poetry is the subject.

Children love rhyme and meter, as we recall from our early days when we jumped rope or insulted each other with simple verses, some of which go back hundreds of years and have been passed on orally from one generation to the next. Some of us lucky ones, though we may have hated the idea at the time, were forced to memorize poems and recite them as we fidgeted in front of our classmates, by old-fashioned teachers who knew their stuff. Now, when we're trapped in the dentist's office or standing in line at the checkout counter, we can pass the time by reciting in our heads "The Lake Isle of Inisfree," or searching for the second stanza of "Invictus"—aided of course by rhyme and meter.

The first poem I learned by heart on my own was Gertrude Stein's "Grass":

Be cool inside the mule
Be cool inside the mule
Be cool inside with a monkey tied
Be cool inside the mule.

I was five years old. I loved the incantation, and the strangeness, even as it baffled my literal-minded elders.

You'd think, from the way some people carry on, that rhyme and meter were imposed on poetry by ancient, dried-up academicians with long beards and quill pens, instead of being the result of deep and primitive impulses: chanting, foot-stamping and beating with a stick on an old tin pot. Then the joys of discovering that a word chimes with other words; the joys of repetition that can send us into a kind of ecstatic trance:

I know a little cupboard
With a teeny tiny key,
And there's a jar of Lollypops
For me, me, me.

That's a stanza from Walter de la Mare, whose magic poems are once again available in a number of recent collections of verse for children. Oh, it's *me, me, me* that children love. The separation from Mother takes a few turbulent years of scuffling and grabbing—"Gimme that! It's mine, *mine!*"—to achieve the autonomous self.

The Dick-and-Jane syndrome, which preached the utility of monosyllables, pasteurized childhood, that time of all times when we are ruled by passion, hilarity and instant tears. Walter de la Mare never forgot this, nor our love of the spooky, the scary, the mysterious:

A mouse in the wainscot is nibbling;
A wind in the keyhole drones;
And a sheet webbed over my candle, Susie,
Grill me some bones!

56

(That stanza is from "At the Keyhole," in the *Oxford Book of Poetry for Children*, edited by Edward Blishen and vividly Illustrated by Brian Wildsmith. The selections are all by English persons, including some unusual choices such as John Clare and Osbert Sitwell.)

Vachel Lindsay, a poet now thoroughly out of fashion, still speaks to children. "The Moon's the North Wind's Cookie" is widely anthologized. My own children wore out the records on which Burl Ives sang some of Lindsay's poems, including this one:

> *There was a little turtle*
> *He lived in a box*
> *He swam in a puddle*
> *He climbed on the rocks*
>
> *He snapped at a mosquito*
> *He snapped at a flea*
> *He snapped at a minnow*
> *And he snapped at me*
>
> *He caught the mosquito*
> *He caught the flea*
> *He caught the minnow*
> *But he didn't catch me.*

"Yah, yah, yah! Can't catch me!" Like Lindsay, Theodore Roethke never forgot what it was to be young. Like many poets, they both stayed part child to the very end. Roethke was a friend to my children and me—and I can hear still his deep, growly voice reciting to them:

> *There Once was a Cow with a Double Udder.*
> *When I think of it now, I just have to shudder!*

Roethke's children's book, *I Am Says the Lamb*, with its delicious illustrations by Robert Leydenfrost, has gone out of

57

print, but in his *Collected Poems* there are grown-up poems that suit the young very well, like "My Papa's Waltz," "Vernal Sentiment" (with its clickety rhythms like a rapid typist) and "Night Journey" (with its quiet love for the American landscape).

When I was a child I carried around with me a small green volume called "Sing Song," by Christina Rossetti. I still carry many of her poems around in my head, like this one with its gentle moral message, all too relevant today:

> *My clothes are soft and warm,*
> *Fold upon fold,*
> *But I'm so sorry for the poor*
> *Out in the cold.*

This Rossetti poem can be found in the *Oxford Book*, along with four others:

> *Hopping frog, hop here and be seen,*
> *I'll not pelt you with stick or stone:*
> *Your cap is laced and your coat is green;*
> *Goodbye, we'll let each other alone.*

A poem like this—and another of her poems, also untitled, that begins "Hurt no living thing"—is an antidote to what children pick up from television. And who is to supply the antidote if not we parents and grandparents—especially those of us who, fortunately, were read to ourselves?

Of course we adults miss a good deal of the joy of reading if we leave the choice of poems to the anthologists when we could be leafing through wonderful works ourselves. Robert Frost and Emily Dickinson especially come to mind. However, for the benefit of busy and lazy parents, here are some poems repeatedly tested on numerous children of my acquaintance: Robert Frost's "Good Hours," "The Last Word of a Bluebird," "Dust of Snow" and "The Pasture," as well as the ones we all know, "Stopping by Woods on a Snowy Evening" and "The Road Not Taken."

As for Miss D. (you'll remember that her poems have numbers, not titles, so I quote first lines): "Hope is the thing with feathers," "A Bird came down the Walk" ("He did not know I saw / He bit an Angleworm in halves / And ate the fellow, raw"), "The Grass so little has to do" (which concludes with that glorious line, "I wish I were a Hay!"). And her poem that begins, "You cannot put a Fire out," and concludes, "You cannot fold a Flood / And put it in a drawer / Because the Winds would find it out / And tell your Cedar floor." (Children still know that all inanimate objects are really alive and whisper to us at night when we are in bed.)

There are two good anthologies for children with poems chosen by Jack Prelutsky. I prefer *Read Aloud Rhymes for the Very Young* (Knopf) to *The Random House Book of Poetry for Children*, both because the illustrations by Marc Brown are adorable and because it isn't arranged by theme. I don't believe that children want to hear five or six consecutive poems about snow; they'd rather hop around. Also, a much higher proportion of the poems in the "Read-Aloud" book are by living American poets, fine ones like some of those already mentioned as well as Maxine Kumin, Gwendolyn Brooks, Stanley Kunitz and Lucille Clifton, as well as Eve Merriam and X.J. Kennedy (both fine children's anthologists). Another beautiful book (I've given away as many copies as I could find) is *A Child's Treasury of Poems* (Dial), edited by Mark Daniel, illustrated with 50 paintings in color from the Victorian and Edwardian eras. *Talking to the Sun* (Henry Holt), a less orthodox selection by Kenneth Koch, has gorgeous, splashy illustrations by Kate Farrell.

It's a sound idea to avoid anthologies called "The World's Greatest" or "The Hundred Best," which tend to cobble together elderly, out-of-print poems, some of them too tired to stand alone. However, this does not mean that some of the old standbys should be ignored: anything by that Peter Pan of authors, Robert Louis Stevenson; Walt Whitman's "O Captain! My Captain!"; Alfred Noyes's "Highwayman," and that raven of E. A. Poe. But you remember those, don't you?

An Essay on Failure: A Commencement Address

Greetings to you, graduates. This is a day when you receive congratulations from all sides—your teachers, relatives and friends. And amid the hugs, the flowers, the tears of pride and parting, come the heartfelt wishes for your *success*.

Today you are given a piece of paper—formerly a sheepskin—which officially attests to your success. It's beautiful, it's official, and it bears the signature of the President of your University. Some of you may even frame it. Forgive me for saying so, but this may be the last tangible proof of success—signed, beribboned and delivered with due pomp—that you will ever have. From now on, success is up to you, and the truest criteria of that success will be internal: how you feel about yourselves—the degree to which you have fulfilled your early promise. Promise! There's a word for you: "I promise to be good." "I promise to be better." We say these earliest promises to our mother and father. Our later promises are to ourselves, sometimes with grim determination, sometimes with despair. I will be a credit to those who believe in me. I *will* succeed!

And now comes the bad news: You may become rich—but, as the examples of Wall Street arbitrageurs and the likes of Donald Trump and Lee Iacocca show us, never rich enough. You may be happy, but perhaps never as completely happy as you are at this hour. And, by your own terms, you will fail. You will fail at marriage, because in some respects it will not live up to your idealistic expectations. Some of you, most of you, have had love affairs or experiments in love and sharing. So I don't need to tell you that when these relationships break up, you experience the bitterness of failure. If you have hurt the other person more than he or she has hurt you, that too you experience as failure: failure in kindness, failure in understanding, failure to be responsible for your own actions—which can be other names for cruelty, intended or not.

When and if you marry, statistics tell us that half of all marriages today end in divorce. That too is bitter beyond imagining. So roughly half of you will castigate yourselves for failures in judgment (you picked the wrong person), in patience, intuition and compromise. If you stay married, it will be less satisfactory than your expectations, as I have said. You will probably become parents. Not long ago, I was interviewed by a young theoretical psychoanalyst, for a book she is writing about the parent-child relationship. In the course of the interview I remarked with a sigh that I felt like a failure as a parent. "Oh," she replied with a kindly smile, "*all* parents think that." And this was comforting, in a way. Your parents out there, flushed with pride and considerably lighter in pocketbook, relieved that you made it, still have their regrets. You grew up so quickly! They didn't spend enough of what is now called "quality time" with you. They didn't listen to you—your hints of problems or unhappiness—as long or as carefully as they should have. And now you have flown the coop!

Despite what I have just said, these are not counsels of gloom and doom—quite the contrary. Welcome failure! For success teaches us nothing. In fact, it may lead us seriously astray. We may become puffed up, as the Bible puts it. Sometimes we may become so puffed up that we explode, and are never heard from again except in pathetic bits and pieces. A lesser danger is that we may begin to take seriously what the media says about us, and believe that we can get away with

62

slipshod or careless work, where once we took infinite pains. As a writer who also reads, I can assure you that once writers achieve fame, they can print any piece of garbage they like in newspapers, magazines or books. And they seldom stop to reflect that they are subverting the very reputation that they have struggled so long and hard to achieve.

But the really great people of our time are modest people. Einstein, Gandhi, Mother Teresa. And believe me, all of these people thought of themselves, or think of themselves, as failures. Take Tolstoi, whom many of us believe to have been one of the greatest novelists who ever lived. He ended up trying to be a shoemaker—perhaps the worst shoemaker who ever picked up a tack hammer and a piece of leather. Take that great thinker, Simone Weil, who turned to factory work as a kind of penance, so clumsy that she injured herself repeatedly, becoming so ill because of overwork and self-starvation that she died, still a young woman.

Einstein said that if he had his life to live over again, he would be a carpenter. When Gandhi was gunned down by a fanatic, his last thoughts must have been of his failure to bring religious harmony to his people. And in the India of today, tragically, hardly a trace remains of that most noble of experiments. Mother Teresa experiences failure every day, every hour, often every few minutes, as she holds a dying man or woman in her arms, because all of Gandhi's efforts, all of her own efforts, have not improved the conditions of the desperately poor by one iota. And yet these are the truly great, whose names will live as long as history exists.

But though we do not agree with the harsh appraisals they have made of themselves, if we read their biographies, study their lives, we learn that they grew, matured and achieved by a series of failures. The career of a scientist is the clearest illustration of this: When a laboratory experiment fails for the umpteenth time, does this man or woman go home and put his or her head in the oven? Indeed not. It's back to the test tube and the drawing board, with the knowledge that another

63

avenue has proved to be a dead end, and that by this process of elimination, one is that much closer to fulfillment of the dream.

So welcome failure! If we adopt the calm approach of the scientist in the face of temporary defeat, we will not bang our heads against the wall, curse our spouses and kick the dog. More important, we will not castigate ourselves for our short-comings or allow ourselves to be overcome by a sense of self-worthlessness. This is the most strenuous exercise in futility that I can think of.

Instead, when a relationship goes on the rocks, we will not denounce human folly, particularly our own, and vow that never again will we allow ourselves to become so open, so intimately involved, so vulnerable to hurt. That isn't just the coward's way; it's the way to insulate ourselves from growth and become emotional hermits—God forbid.

When an investment, emotional or financial, fails, we will re-animate that cliché about experience being the great teacher and prove it to be so, by striving to become *more* involved, *more* sensitive to the needs of others, next time.

With those we love, we will concentrate more on what we can give them rather than what they can give us. Do I sound preachy? How did I get so smart? you may well ask. I say to you in all humility: through doomed experiments, bad poems, and a first marriage that was a spectacular failure. I learned from stupid choices, from wise children—many of them my students—that I didn't respond to as fully as I should have; and from the death of parents who still had much to teach me if only I had listened, if only I had remembered to ask, while there was still time.

Professionally, I have had some modest success. Other-wise, I wouldn't be up here, right? And let me be frank: What I fear most today is not that I will fail, but that I will fail and not know it. As long as we have that uneasy feeling that we can do better than we are doing, we are in good shape. As long as we are haunted by what we have left undone, or should never have done in the first place, there is hope for you and even me. But how about a little peace and quiet now and then? How about resting on those laurels, or that one measly laurel, from time to time? Fine. But just let me say that complacency as a customary state of mind leads to brainrot and the premature death of the imagination. And complacency of a whole people leads to the destruction of the body politic. Our freedom as a nation is a fragile thing; if our democracy is faltering, *its* failure is one that we cannot and must not accept. We must be swift to denounce complacency at the top, and support those leaders who have acquired wisdom from repeated experiments that didn't pan out, who have sympathy for their fellow men and women who are hungry and homeless because they themselves have experienced pain and defeat and thus are committed to helping and healing others.

Our hearts go out to the students of China, whose tragic failure we have witnessed on our television sets these past weeks. But remember: this failure is not an end but a beginning.

So as I close, let me give another feeble cheer for failure. May you confront it with grace without losing hope. May you learn from it life's greatest gift, which is to be fully human.

Eastern Washington University, June 9, 1989

Section V

JAPANESE
FICTION

Donald Keene
and Japanese Fiction

I

Thirty-three years ago Donald Keene edited the *Anthology of Japanese Literature* (Grove Press, 1955) which was "the first comprehensive collection of the riches of Japanese writing ever offered in English," according to *The New Yorker*, dedicated, appropriately enough, to Arthur Waley, whose translation of *The Tale of Genji* was virtually the only work of Japanese literature (other than a handful of poems) known to Western readers until then. Around the same time, American film buffs—those fortunate enough to live in towns with art houses, as they were then called—were stunned by the film, *Rashōmon* (made in 1950 but distributed in the U.S. considerably later). It was, of course, directed by Kurosawa and based on two stories by Ryunosuke Akutagawa, a writer famous in Japan but unknown to us. Then began the spate of Japanese stories, novels and films which have affected not only our own aesthetic perceptions but our appreciation of Japanese culture in almost every area: architecture, flower arranging, the tea ceremony, the theater of Nōh, Kabuki and the Bunraku puppets, judo, karate and Zen Buddhism, not to mention Japanese cuisine. (It's amusing to note, in translations from this era, the careful explanation of the words for

69

Japanese articles of apparel, and food such as sushi—words that joined our vocabulary some time ago.)

Dr. Keene followed his first book a year later with *Modern Japanese Literature* (also Grove Press), and in the preface to that work explained why the second volume, covering a period of eighty years or so, was as long as the previous one, which encompassed a thousand years. "All the literature which survives from, say, the thirteenth century can hardly compare in bulk with what any single year now produces. But it is not only by mere numbers that modern Japanese literature earns the right to be heard: its quality is remarkably high, and compares with that written anywhere in the world." Any thought that this might be hyperbole—enthusiasm to which Dr. Keene is not prone—was quickly dispelled by reading stories by Kawabata Yasunari and Dazai Osamu, episodes from longer works of Tanizaki Junichirō, and an excerpt from the novel, *Confession of a Mask*, by the very young (twenty-four) Mishima Yukio—to mention only the most familiar names.

This extraordinary prose was matched by the equally high quality of the translations—by names which have become familiar and honored over the years: Burton Watson, Edward Seidensticker, Theodore deBary, the late Ivan Morris and of course Keene himself. We owe a debt of gratitude to the Japanese for attacking us at Pearl Harbor, for some of these translators as gifted students were scooped up by the U.S. Navy and thrust into Japanese language schools at Berkeley, Boulder and Columbia before being shipped overseas to interrogate prisoners and decipher the diaries and letters of the dead. The list of works which these men—and in recent years their students, including women like Karen Brazell and Mildred Tahara—have made available to us is too long to cite here, but it is a rich and brilliant outpouring. And very recently Donald Keene has given us a full account of the lives and works of these writers and many more still awaiting translation, an account which occupied him for more than fifteen years. It is called *Dawn to the West*, and it is a staggering enterprise. Because of its vast length—the first volume devoted to novelists runs to 1327 pages—and its $60 price tag, it is to be feared that the book has been read mainly by scholars in the field rather than by the general reader for whom it was intended, so it seems appropriate here to summarize and comment on its content.

It is difficult to imagine that this study of prose from the Meiji Restoration (1868) to the present will ever be superseded: Keene is not only the preeminent authority in Japanese studies; happily for us, he writes with a limpid ease and deadpan wit all too rare in scholarly writing. The book is so arranged that it may be read as a sort of encyclopedia as well as a sustained narrative (though I will stick to the latter approach in writing about it). Each chapter is autonomous; thus, a certain amount of essential information is repeated, so that the reader is not obliged to search out other references in the index in regard to a specific author or literary movement.

Though many accounts of literary movements are thrust into a Procrustean time frame for the sake of convenience, in this case there is a definite date for the beginning of the modern literary movement. It began with the commencement of the Meiji Restoration, after the new Emperor announced that Japan would henceforth reach out to the rest of the world to promote the national welfare. To summarize what happened next, Keene tells us that "Japanese who studied abroad were expected to devote themselves to chemistry, public hygiene, agriculture and other useful varieties of learning. Most of those who became interested in foreign literature did so by accident." Sometimes they learned a foreign language from a work of literature because there were no proper textbooks; sometimes, "a Japanese student about to return home would be given a work of literature as a farewell present by a foreign friend."

The first wave of translations by Japanese of foreign

authors was not always of works of significance, the books having been acquired so randomly, "but without these translations the new Japanese literature could not have developed so quickly or so successfully." One smiles a little to learn that Bulwer-Lytton was frequently translated and highly esteemed. Zola had a remarkable influence; he was translated by writers whose own proclivities might be compared to, say, Ronald Firbank, Theodore Dreiser and Henry James. One result was that a Japanese version of "Naturalism" had a quite disproportionate influence. Some misconceptions of Western literary movements were due to a certain amount of creativity on the part of Japanese whose comprehension of Western languages was less than perfect. (However, it should be pointed out that Western versions of Oriental works well into the twentieth century were equally "creative" and inaccurate; in fact one suspects that the whole concept of the "Mysterious East" arose from problems of communication rather than any inherent obscurity.)

Naturally, the Japanese had hoped to import only the finest flowers of Western civilization, but as we know to our sorrow, it doesn't work that way. Keene says that the slogan, "Combine the best of East and West" was often invoked, "but in practice it was easier to combine the worst of East and West, as we know, say, from the wood block prints . . . with their garish purples, greens, and carmines that were the products of European dyes. . . ."

Only well into modern times were works of literature written in colloquial Japanese. Traditionally, nearly all books were written, if not in Chinese, in classical Japanese, "an artificial language that no one had spoken for many hundreds of years." This language was difficult to understand but, Keene tells us, "it had acquired a special dignity and resonance, which gave pleasure even to illiterates who enjoyed hearing passages read aloud." In a transitional phase, works were written partly in traditional, partly in colloquial language, especially the conversations. Finally, in this century,

72

classical Japanese was renounced by the novelists—not by the poets, who may write in it to this day.

Chinese was gradually abandoned as the language of the Samurai class after Japan defeated China in the Sino-Japanese war of 1894-'95, and her troops surrendered with what the Japanese considered as shameful ease. China, once the acme of world civilization, had shown herself to be vulnerable. The nationalism aroused by this war led to the shift to Japanese as the language of higher learning, instead of English, as formerly. This may have been a factor in the Japanese' notorious difficulty in mastering other languages, although it did lead to a greater appreciation of native literature and learning.

During the next thirty or thirty-five years, Japanese literature, whatever its school, developed an extraordinary fusion of elements from East and West. Perhaps the most important influence of Western thought was to introduce the concept of romantic love, and with it, the discovery of the individual, followed closely by the idea that literature could be the vehicle for political ideas. However, the rise of militarism in the early thirties meant the suppression of leftist and proletarian writings. Communist writers were arrested, tortured, and forced to renounce their beliefs; this enforced conversion, called *tenkō*, sometimes inspired confessional novels. Later, patriotic effusions, largely worthless, were produced by many of the *tenkō* writers. Serious literature more or less came to a halt during the China war, and the Pacific war which overlapped it. However, with the end of the war, and the Occupation, many Japanese writers were free to speak as they chose for the first time in their lives. Many of the finest works are postwar recollections. The public, starved for reading matter during the long years of war, flocked to the bookstores, and read voraciously, not only the new Japanese works but the European literature long denied them. To this day the Japanese read far more works in translation than the people of any other nation, and it has been said that one

73

would have greater access to world literature through a knowledge of Japanese than that of any other single language.

And the translators, in the immediate postwar period, many of them members of the Occupation forces, turned to the translation of the new novels, short stories and poetry. The Japanese film industry, spurred by the presence of a handful of geniuses, Kurasawa the first to be brought to our attention, moved into the international spotlight. And this is where we came in.

*   *   *   *   *

Before I began to read Professor Keene's book, I assumed that I would be most interested in learning more about the lives and beliefs of writers with whom I was most familiar. This did not prove to be the case. I defy any nation to come up with a list of more eccentric, even bizarre, writers than those discussed here. One is left with the impression that they either committed suicide rather early in life, or lived to be ninety! However, there are exceptions, including some noted authors not widely known in the West:

Natsume Sōseki (1867-1916), popularly believed to be the greatest writer of the modern period, was one of eight children. Bounced back and forth between his overburdened parents and foster homes, he grew so confused about the identity of his real family that he took his parents to be his grandparents. This is no doubt one cause of the hypersensitivity which developed into near-paranoia as he grew older. A brilliant child, he was especially proficient in Chinese studies as well as English, although he disliked English at first. However, he became convinced that a brilliant career lay in English studies rather than anything else. He was the second man to graduate from Tokyo University with a degree in English literature, after having written a dazzling paper on Whitman—Whitman's initial appearance in Japan. However, even after Sōseki became an established writer, his ambivalence about the West lingered on. He fled from an unhappy marriage (which also seems to be standard among Japanese male writers) to England in 1900, where he spent two years. (His tutor in English was an Irishman, so it's probable that he spoke English with a brogue!) Sōseki kept to himself, made no friends, and "became convinced as the result of his dealings with landladies and tradesmen that he had previously held the English in exaggerated respect," says Keene. He was left with a dislike for England, even English literature, and particularly for the spirit of materialism and devotion to money which he saw being imported into Japan. Racism was another factor: the English made him feel insignificant, and he says that when he caught a glimpse of his own face reflected in a shop window he burst into laughter.

When he returned to Japan, he succeeded Lafcadio Hearn as a lecturer at Tokyo University. Hearn's dismissal was a result of the rising spirit of nationalism. Many of us will groan to learn that the first course he taught was an appreciation of *Silas Marner*. The student reaction was predictable, and when Sōseki was able to teach Shakespeare's plays the following year, it must have been a great relief to all. Sōseki was also the first serious critic of English literature in Japan; his criticism included psychological and philosophical analyses as well. However, he was embittered by the realization that, no matter how brilliant his criticism, he would never be taken seriously in England. This bitterness, his sense of unease and alienation, his black moods and his domestic misery continued throughout his life, and darkened the work of his later years. One cannot help but feel that his lifelong seesaw between East and West, China and America, his love-hate relationship with England and America, contributed to his unhappiness. Dr. Keene speculates on the turn his life might have taken had he spent those two crucial years in Peking rather than London.

Some readers will remember with pleasure the first chapter of Sōseki's early novel, *Botchan,* in *Modern Japanese Literature,* translated by Burton Watson. It is his most popular work in Japan, and it is easy to see why. Botchan (his name means something approximating "Sonny Boy") is a naive, generous-spirited, not overly bright young man who goes to be a teacher on the island of Shikoku; he is surrounded by people—fellow-teachers, relatives, friends—considerably less appealing than he, to put it mildly. There is a sunny charm which permeates this work which, along with his first published work, *I Am a Cat*, a story written from the cat's point of view, has a playfulness and gently satiric spirit (although this becomes more sardonic as *I Am a Cat* continues) which gives way to less colloquial, more poetic and increasingly dismal works. Although all of his writing has been well-received and respectfully treated on the part of the Japanese public, critical opinion has been divided. Tanizaki, for example, tore the last novel, *Light and Darkness*, limb from limb. But still, in these late works, one must respect his honesty, his lack of pretense, his scorn for materialism and nationalism. He died of tuberculosis, leaving *Light and Darkness* (which is regarded by some as his supreme achievement) unfinished, but composing poetry in Japanese and Chinese right to the end.

Mori Ōgai (1862-1922) is usually paired with Sōseki when Japan's leading modern writers are mentioned, although they attract rather different readers. Sōseki is revered as a humanist, while Ōgai is admired for what Keene calls his "serene Apollonian manner and his profound respect for Japanese tradition . . . a Samurai through and through." Like Sōseki Ōgai's lifespan is relatively normal, and his private life rather unexceptional. Ōgai grew up in a small town, the eldest son of a physician; he was trained in the Confucian classics and in martial arts. When he was ten, the family moved to Tokyo, where he began studying German, in preparation for his subsequent medical studies. Like William Carlos Williams—although two writers could hardly be more unlike—he pursued twin careers, as an eminent physician (he became Surgeon General of the Japanese army) and as a successful writer. As soon as he received his medical degree from Tokyo University, he went into the army as a medical officer, as was appropriate to one of his samurai antecedents. In 1884 he was sent to Germany to continue his medical studies, where he read widely in German and European literature while taking courses in public hygiene for four years. Unlike Sōseki, Keene says, "Ōgai enjoyed his life abroad, no doubt because he was financially able to take advantage of the amenities of life in Europe, but in part also because he lived as an officer, not as a scholar in dingy lodgings."

When he returned to Japan, Ōgai helped found a literary magazine, *Omokage* (*Vestiges*), which specialized in translations of European poetry, and which was important as a source of the burgeoning Romantic movement. Despite the austerity and understatement of his style, Ōgai was the leading exponent of European Romanticism. Of his three early stories, one concerns a Japanese law student in Berlin, who falls in love with a German dancer. Ultimately, he gives up the girl, who goes mad as a result, in order to pursue a successful career in Japan. At the end, although he doesn't regret his decision, he castigates himself for abandoning his love, in the best German romantic tradition. The second story tells of a Japanese painter who falls in love with a Munich model; the plot involves the mad king of Bavaria, and comes to a suitably lurid and tragic conclusion. It seems clear that the third story, involving a shepherd who is obsessed by a princess, a princess who will not agree to a loveless marriage, and a Japanese officer who acts as a liegeman to a mysterious tragic lady, owes a good deal to the influence of Hans Christian Andersen. Ōgai's loving and careful translation of Andersen's novel *Improvisatoren* into exquisite Japanese influenced more than one generation of Japanese writers; this story of the love of an Italian poet for a beautiful singer is still more widely read in Japan than in Andersen's own country.

This phase of Ōgai's life came to an abrupt halt when the Sino-Japanese War broke out, and Ōgai was sent to the front in 1894. When Ōgai returned to Japan, he got into trouble with his superiors by his advocacy of modern standards of public hygiene, so he was posted to a remote area in Kyushu. He was again sent to the front when the Russo-Japanese War started in 1904. His literary career was largely in abeyance until 1909, when he burst forth with his novel, *Vita Sexualis,* fourteen short stories, and a number of translations. Now he switched from classical Japanese to the colloquial, and his typical stories concerned ordinary people in realistic situations. However, *Vita Sexualis* caused a tremendous furor. It was banned as a threat to public morals, although its tone has more in common with a cold shower than with a steam bath. It is the sexual history of a professor who, as a child, is shown pornographic drawings which he doesn't understand, traces his school career when he fends off with a dagger the advances of his schoolmates, to the time when he has a single sexual encounter in a brothel, after which he renounces "animal lust," in vivid contrast to the life of the novelist Nagai Kafū, who more or less took up lifelong residence in houses of prostitution, as will be seen.

Ōgai was married for a year-and-a-half, and then divorced, after which he seems to have enjoyed his bachelor status, which lasted for a dozen years, as indicated by a number of stories written in this period. His second marriage, in 1902, continued to the end of his life, although literary evidence suggests that this marriage also had its ups and downs. Ōgai's wife felt such detestation for a story called "Half a Day," concerning a husband, wife and mother-in-law, three intensely disagreeable characters, that it could not be reprinted until after her death. However, Mishima adored this story, saying that it conveyed a more intense impression of desolation than any work of Naturalist literature depicting the misery of poverty. He said, "Ōgai saw in his own household the failure of Japan's modern age." But Keene warns us to be wary of taking Ōgai's works too literally. "He habitually wore a mask, revealing to his readers only as much of himself as he deemed appropriate." To his admirers this mask, "like a Nōh mask, was a thing of beauty in itself, a dignified, noble abstraction of the man."

Ōgai's first novel, *Youth*, is clearly influenced by Ibsen; one episode in the book takes place at a performance of *John Gabriel Borkman* (in Ōgai's translation); and the unfolding of the plot parallels this work, up to a point when the protagonist, realizing that the Mrs. Wilton-like character hasn't taken him seriously, converts his humiliation and frustration into a passionate desire to write. Ōgai's next major work, *The Wild Goose*, would seem to be a continuation of that influence, although the symbolism seems heavy-handed in comparison to *The Wild Duck*.

The third phase of Ōgai's career was devoted to *shiden*, or biographies, and historical novels. Unlike most studies in this genre—and unlike anything Japan has produced since—the *shiden* are devoted to the lives of obscure men, emphasizing their noble and humane qualities. *Abe Ichizoku* (*The Abe Clan*) is a historical work. The elegant restraint of its prose is captured in Keene's translation of the following passage (the family is being attacked by the overpowering forces of the *daimyo*, and prepare themselves by thoroughly cleaning their house, taking part in a farewell banquet, after which the old people and the women kill themselves, and the children are stabbed to death one by one; the corpses are buried, and only the young men remain):

"Drums and gongs had sounded all night long inside the stronghold, but now it was so silent it seemed to be empty. The gate was chained shut and a spider's thread hung from the tip of the branch of a tall oleander, which grew two or three feet higher than the board fence. Beads of night dew shone like pearls along the thread. A swallow flew up from somewhere and darted within the wall."

Keene ends his chapter on Ōgai by saying that Ōgai exemplifies the best in the Japanese tradition of soldier-scholars. "He had no disciples. . . . His reputation however, has continued to grow since his death in 1922, a tribute not only to the man himself but to the Japanese reading public."

Nagai Kafū (1879-1959) is one of the more fascinating eccentrics in a field where he has some keen competition. Born into a cosmopolitan household, where the Confucian classics were stressed, along with the trappings of Western civilization such as tablecloths, chairs and European cuisine, he was able to adjust to French and American manners during his sojourn in the West with an easy confidence rare among his contemporaries. His father, although he considered himself a man of the Enlightenment, was a rigid Confucian, with some eccentricities of his own. Edward Seidensticker tells us that the father would not allow melons in the house because he thought that they were vulgar. (Keene's book sent me to re-reading Seidensticker's marvelous life of the poet, *Kafū the Scribbler*, published by Stanford in 1965.) Owing to his background, Kafū was something of a snob, showing contempt for provincial Japanese (although his parents had emigrated to Tokyo from the country), which may have been another bond he had with the Parisians when he went to France. When Kafū reviewed Tanizaki's *The Makioka Sisters* (which is situated in Osaka and environs) he pretended to find the characters as exotic as those in D'Annunzio.

Kafū was one of the devotees of Zola mentioned earlier, also a rather improbable one, given his enthusiasm for the beauties of nature and women, especially the charms of waitresses, prostitutes and dancing girls. He was attracted by Zola's emphasis on environment and heredity in the formation of character. Also, "Zola's bold rejection of the literature of the past suited me perfectly . . . everybody was crying out against the old assumptions," he wrote later. His infatuation with French literature lasted to the end of his life, long after he had abandoned Zola for more esoteric authors.

Kafū's first novels, *Ambition* and *The Flowers of Hell*, both came out in 1902. Keene tells us that "Even in his youth Kafū lacked Zola's burning convictions; his exposure of the ruthless ambitions of a young Meiji businessman was in keeping with his scorn for everything associated with the Meiji era and its ideals, a condemnation of bad taste rather than of social evil." *The Flowers of Hell* is more concerned with the effects of heredity and environment, although the influence of Ibsen and—I would guess—Gissing is evident: Ibsen in the sub-theme involving an educated woman's struggle for independence, Gissing in the depiction of characters from the comfortable strata of society who are drawn to the lower depths.

Kafū's third novel, *The Woman of the Dream*, has a mood closer to Maupassant's *Une Vie* than anything by Zola. Keene suggests that he had already fallen under the spell of the only foreign author he would openly acknowledge as his master. Seidensticker says of it, "Against a background of autumnal landscapes, chilly houses, and feckless men incapable of love, sometimes incapable of conversation, the life of a woman unfolds."

Footloose and feckless, having been expelled from school for non-attendance, having experimented with apprenticeships in music and theater to the consternation of his family, fired from his job on a newspaper, Kafū was the despair of his parents, even though his novels had achieved modest success. So, in the time-honored tradition of upper-class fathers— and not in Japan alone—Kafū was shipped abroad. He was supposed to study English and acquire some knowledge of business. He ended up in Tacoma, Washington, of all places, where he promptly signed up for courses in high school French. He spent a year in Seattle, moved on to St. Louis for the fair, and then went to Michigan, where he enrolled in Kalamazoo College, and polished his French. He was to boast that by the time he left America his French was better than his English.

Finally Kafū got a job working for the New York branch of a Yokohama bank, where he was employed until 1907, still mad to get to France, and saving his money to that end. During his American stay he wrote the stories that were eventually published as *Tales of America*. I would give a good deal to read those stories set in Tacoma and Seattle, my native heath, but they have not as yet been translated. Unlike most Japanese in the United States in this period, Kafū saw our country with an unprejudiced eye. "He was attracted especially by the relations that prevailed between young men and women, and described with evident envy how college students walked together hand in hand to chapel, or how an engaged couple played music together." He was also pleased to encounter a young woman who asked him if he liked opera; he was crazy about it, in fact, and regularly attended the Met at a time when Caruso sang every week. This conversation moved him to tears: "I confess that I like Western women. Nothing gives me more pleasure than conversing with Western women about Western art from the time of the Greeks, whether we speak in English or French, as long as it is a Western language, under a Western sky, by a Western body of water."

Although he grew more ambivalent about America in later life, he never forgot this girl and the happiness he felt with her in America. Kafū married twice, both times unsuccessfully because of his compulsive promiscuity. "He also had innumerable liaisons with geishas, prostitutes, waitresses and other women available for money, but never again with a woman who could discuss with him music or the beauty of lights at sea." (Keene.) Kafū also enjoyed New York's Chinatown; it wasn't the cuisine or the garish souvenirs which attracted him but "the tenements on the back alleys— an exhibition gallery of vices, shame, disease and death so extreme that surely human beings cannot sink any lower . . . It is a treasure trove for *Les fleurs du mal*. I only fear that the so-called humanitarian charities may in the end sweep this special world from its corner of society."

Finally, Kafū made it to France! He wrote a companion to the American book called *Tales of France*. His happiness there was flawed by the presence of his fellow-countrymen, whom he avoided when he could. Keene remarks that "it is hard to think of any other Japanese writer who so consistently wrote unfriendly comments about his countrymen," and his misanthropy became more pronounced with the years. He tore himself from France with the greatest reluctance. Why couldn't he live and die in Paris like Heine, Turgenev, Chopin and the rest? In Singapore, on the way home, he mused, "The East is really unspeakable. I felt that this is where heavy drudgery begins." Ah, Paris! In Paris, "men shave every morning. People polish their nails. At mealtime wine and music are indispensable, etc., etc." He takes out a volume of Musset. But the purser interrupts, to present him to a Japanese family. He finds them horrible. The father sports a mustache that projects to left and right like a shrimp's antennae; his son has a face like an octopus and a perpetually runny nose; the wife nurses the child openly while he pees on her kimono; she is seasick before the ship begins to move. The essay in which this account occurs concludes: "I recalled a line of Verlaine and asked this land of Japan, 'Have I been born too soon? Or too late?'" The book on France was banned for immorality, although it's hard to see what upset the censors. Kafū was home.

And he stayed in Japan until he died, fifty years later, continuously productive, pouring out novels and stories, most of them set in the milieux he preferred: the world of the demimonde, of geishas of high degree, prostitutes common and uncommon, actors and musicians, down to waitresses in cheap cafés who sold themselves to customers to eke out their meager incomes. Although his style, Keene says, is beautiful, at once clear and evocative, "a glory of modern Japanese literature," he has never been ranked as highly by critics as he deserves, "if only because his works do not require elaborate commentary and seem rarely to take themselves seriously," two fatal shortcomings so far as critics are concerned.

Readers may remember with pleasure his story, "The River Sumida" (in *Modern Japanese Literature*) the story of a boy who is drawn to the world of the theater. The young girl he loves is becoming a geisha. But his mother has made terrible sacrifices to send him to school. The boy, Chōkichi, in despair, stays out in a rainstorm when he has a cold, hoping to catch pneumonia. The boy's uncle, a noted haiku master, has refused to involve himself on behalf of the boy until it is almost too late, and Chōkichi is desperately ill. Keene finds the end of the story curiously sentimental: the uncle swears to stand by the boy, help him become an actor, and see that he gets the girl. But I find the ending more ambiguous, more "Japanese" (as we conceive that atmosphere) than this. I quote the ending from Keene's own translation: "Another mouse suddenly raced over the ceiling. The wind was still blowing, and the flame in the hanging lamp quivered continually. Like some illustrator of romances thinking of pictures for a book, Ragetsu over and over drew in his mind the portraits of the two young, beautiful people—Chōkichi with his fair skin, delicate face, and clear eyes; and Oito with her charming mouth and tilted eyes set in a round face. And he cried in his heart, 'No matter how bad your fever is, don't die! Chōkichi, there's nothing to worry about. I am with you.'" It seems to me just as probable that Chōkichi *will* die, and that everyone else will live unhappily ever after. This story is not typical of Kafū, the hedonist; unfortunately, so little of his work has been translated into English that we are left with descriptions of work rather than the work itself. Onwards, translators!

Kafū refused to support the war effort from 1937 to 1945, for which all honor to him. He published very little during these years; the government considered him frivolous, and editors were wary. Keene says that "his fondness for describing women of the demi-monde, rather than heroic women who inspire their sons and husbands to do battle, led the authorities to judge that he was their enemy, and they were right." He filled his diary with "expressions of contempt for the militarists and their policies." He went on writing nonetheless, and when the war was finally over had accumulated a fine backlog, which shot him into prominence once more. But he became increasingly eccentric and reclusive. Let our last and characteristic glimpse of him be as he strolls along a narrow street in "the gay quarter," with a giggling chorus girl on either arm.

*   *   *   *   *

Brief mention must be made of a writer whose output is meager compared to the other writers discussed here—Arishima Takeo (1877-1923)—for two reasons: first, his extraordinary novel, *A Certain Woman*, and second, his suicide, both to have repercussions. Like Kafū, Arishima came from a cosmopolitan family; his father, too, believed that Japanese must adapt themselves to Western customs and manners. Arishima, as a small child, was sent to stay with an American family in Yokohama, and by the age of seven he was enrolled in a mission school where most of his fellow students were foreigners and English was the language of instruction. The Christian bias of this institution was to affect Arishima in ways that his father, a minor samurai, could not have foreseen. But at ten the boy was sent to the Peer's School, where he was such a model of deportment that he was allowed to play with the Crown Prince. Nine years later Arishima chose to enter the Sapporo Agricultural School, partly because of his distaste for things military and partly due to a vision he had of becoming an enlightened landed proprietor. Arishima lived with the family of Nitobe Inazō, the scholarly Japanese Quaker who later achieved fame as Japan's first great internationalist. A close relationship with a fellow student, compounded in equal parts of religious aspiration and homosexuality—or so says Kenneth Strong, translator of *A Certain Woman*, in his introduction to that book—led him, after much spiritual torment, to become a convert to Christianity. At the same time, and quite naturally, he began to evince an interest in socialism. On a visit to the family land in Hokkaido, Strong says, "the servility of the tenants made him want to run away, not in contempt, but in shame at the man-made gap it signified

85

between himself and these fellow human beings." In 1903 Arishima left for America.

In Chicago he visited a friend from the Sapporo school, Mori Hiroshi. Mori had been engaged to a young woman who had agreed to join him in America. But on board ship to America she had conceived a passion for the chief purser, and when the ship docked in Seattle she refused to go ashore, returning to Japan when the ship left port. Mori's account of this traumatic episode was to serve as the basis for the first half of *A Certain Woman*.

Arishima received his M.A. from Haverford and moved on to Harvard, where he stayed with F.W. Peabody, who introduced him to the poetry of Whitman. He was over-whelmed. Later he was to write, "Suddenly, and with aston-ishing force, Whitman's great hand struck me on the shoul-der." He wrote of Whitman as the voice of the coming genera-tion. He left Harvard and went to read at the Library of Congress, mainly the Russians and Scandinavians. Besides Whitman, Tolstoy and Ibsen were to have a lasting effect.

Arishima left America in 1906, to join his brother in Naples, where they haunted the museums, before he moved to London, and there too spent most of his time in the British Museum reading Kropotkin, among others. Then he met Kropotkin: "I forgot that I was in England, that I was a Japanese, and even where in space his study might be situ-ated." "How rare," writes Keene, "were the Japanese of this time or even much later who could forget . . . their national-ity and feel no necessity either to defend or to reject Japan!" In 1907 he went home, and married the following year—unhappily, it almost goes without saying. During the next decade he wrote essays, and a novella, *Descendants of Cain*, which made him famous. His masterpiece, *A Certain Woman*, was published two years later.

Yōko, the heroine, if she may so be called, has certain features in common with Hedda Gabler—though Hedda is a relatively sympathetic character compared to this "arrogant, self-centered, extravagant, vain . . . thoroughly disagreeable woman," as a critic called her—and to Anna Karenina (Arishima had read Tolstoy's novel on the boat returning him to Japan). Keene says that Yōko "is totally unlike any previous heroine of modern Japanese fiction—strong-willed, decisive in her actions though capricious, full of intense vitality. Even today she contrasts remarkably with most Japanese women of fiction or reality, but in 1919 she burst on the Japanese literary world with immense force." I would say that as a feminist heroine Yōko leaves a great deal to be desired, but there is no doubt about the good intentions of her author. He states his views forcefully in his essay, "Love, the Ruthless Plunderer" (1920): "One might fairly say that everything in contemporary culture, from politics down to fashioning the smallest wooden bucket, has been devised by the genius of men. Men are the suitable users of these facilities; and if a woman wishes to participate in this culture she must to some degree first turn herself into a man." "There are about the same number of men and women on this planet. If, then, the culture of the globe has been created exclusively to satisfy the demands of the males, it is readily apparent how inadequate the content is." "I approve of the women's rights movement as a means of determining the real demands of women, having first created the scope for women to operate of their own free will . . . But I would hope even more that women will join their strength to create from among themselves feminine geniuses. I pray that there will be women who will look afresh at contemporary culture with truly liberated eyes." To which one can only add, "Amen."

However, this stunning essay, so remarkable for its time and place, was nearly his valedictory as a writer. Torn and conflicted always, having described himself earlier as "a wounded dove, hiding its hurt with its wings," he suffered agonies at being unable to live up to his principles in practice. He had lost his Christian faith. "My life is bound to crumble about me. It *is* crumbling, now, clearly," Strong quotes him as writing, in 1922. His last effectual gesture before the end was to turn over his vast estates in Hokkaido to a cooperative of his tenant farmers. But as he wrote in that same year, "I was born, reared, and educated in a class that was not the proletariat. For that reason I am with respect to [them] an unrelated being. It is absolutely impossible for me to become a member of this newly awakened class, and therefore I have no hopes of becoming one. . . ." Marx and Kropotkin couldn't really help either.

He fell in love with a married woman whose husband threatened them with public exposure and a lawsuit. He swore to make them suffer as long as they lived. Arishima and Akiko, his lady, committed suicide in June, 1923, dying in each other's arms.

Although their death was regarded as a conventional "Love-Suicide" as celebrated in the plays of the great Chikamatsu, it had its effect on other writers, not least on the famous Akutagawa Ryūnosuke who, in one of his own suicide notes, attributed his misery to an affair with a married woman and, also like Arishima, to his regret that he had been unable to free himself from the domination of his (adopted) parents. Death was a sort of solution.

Akutagawa Ryūnosuke (1892-1927) may be the first Japanese author discussed here who is familiar to westerners, although they may not recognize his name. He is the author of a story called "Within a Grove", on which the film *Rashomon* was based. (I regret that Professor Keene didn't include a filmography among his full and fascinating appendices.) He, along with Sōseki and Ōgai, make up a triumvirate which is basic to modern Japanese literature. His stories, widely reprinted, widely translated, are taught in schools without, it is hoped, the suffocating sensations induced by the force-feeding of classics to children. He also was born in Tokyo; seven months after his birth his mother went mad, and remained so until her death, ten years later. Once, when he went to visit, she hit him on the head with her pipe. "But most of the time

88

my mother was an extremely well-behaved lunatic," he wrote in a memoir the year before he died.

Akutagawa was adopted by his maternal uncle, and supposedly had a reasonably happy childhood, although he regretted that his foster parents "had never let him do anything he wanted." The child was a good student, and progressed from Japanese and Chinese classics to de Maupassant, France, Strindberg and Dostoievski while still in high school. He majored in English at Tokyo Imperial University, but was distracted from his studies by an unhappy love affair. At this time he wrote the story, "Rashōmon" (not to be confused with the film, although it opens with a shot of the twelfth-century Rashōmon gate—not, as I recall from the film soundtrack, from a period "lost in the mists of antiquity"). Those of us who saw the film have not forgotten the sight of the old crone plucking hairs from the head of a corpse in order to make a wig she can sell. But this story ends with the desperate man taking shelter at the great gate who rips the rags from the old woman in order to sell them.

The twelfth century was a favorite of Akutagawa's, a time of dreadful chaos and violence, when even the great buildings of the capital were broken up for firewood. His stories brought him early popularity, but possibly for the wrong reasons; his ingenuity, smooth style and the use of surprise endings are, like de Maupassant's, not the qualities for which he should be cherished, but rather his eye for the telling detail, and his ability to delineate character in a line or two. Also, he conspicuously lacked originality, and was dependent on what has been called a mosaic of many source materials. Keene tells of one story, "Death of a Martyr," for which he is indebted to Lamartine, Anatole France, Henri de Regnier, Ōgai's translation of Andersen, Quo Vadis, Hebbel's play Judith and various Japanese works. The story is only ten pages long. One critic suggests that despair over his inability to invent may have been one cause of Akutagawa's suicide.

He wrote a group of historical stories set in Nagasaki at the end of the sixteenth century—the period of greatest Christian influence. Akutagawa treats this material with reverence, seeming to envy the religious faith of the Middle Ages which helped people to resolve the ambiguities of life, the war between egotism and selflessness, ambition and idealism, through divine grace, "not by a careful observance of any code of etiquette." He also wrote a group of stories about the early Meiji era when, Keene says, "fashionable Japanese ladies and gentlemen built themselves homes modeled on Victorian domestic architecture, dressed in Western-style clothes, chatted knowingly about European fashions, and prided themselves on their associations with titled foreigners." Now, less than fifty years later, the Japanese had reverted to their own architecture with perhaps one western-style room, wore kimonos at home, and had few contacts with Europeans. To Akutagawa, this earlier period seemed picturesque.

In the 1920s, Akutagawa's reputation continued to grow as the quality of his stories declined. He became ill and over-tired, the victim of insomnia, stomach cramps, nervous exhaustion, heart palpitations, and other ailments, real and perhaps psychosomatic. His stories became increasingly plot-less and episodic, which caused a rather listless quarrel with Tanizaki, who believed that plot was essential. In an essay, he wrote: "There are . . . works of fiction that are close to poems in prose . . . I do not consider such works to be the highest form of fiction, but in terms of 'purity' they are the 'purest' examples of fiction if only because they lack conventional interest." His fiction at this time revealed the lack of energy required to produce works of complex organization. Writing became more and more difficult.

In addition, his family life was painful and complicated. His story, "Genkaku's Villa," is based on material told him by a nurse in the hospital who was taking care of his brother-in-law; it concerns the mistress of the painter Genkaku, who is dying. She arrives at his house, together with the son she has borne him, intending to care for him in his final days. But an unpleasant nurse, and a hostile grandson of the painter—the same age as the illegitimate boy—make her stay unendurable. The story ends with Genkaku's elaborate funeral; a cousin is riding along in the horse-drawn hearse reading a copy of Liebknecht's *Memoirs*. The intent of this ending, Akutagawa wrote a critic, was to pull the tragedy out of the house into the outside world. "Liebknecht, as you know . . . sighed at times when he recalled his meetings with Marx and Engels. I wanted to cast Liebknecht's mournful shadow over my student (the cousin)."

He labored over this story while another brother-in-law, who had burned down his own house in order to collect the insurance, committed suicide by throwing himself under a train. Akutagawa, who was close to collapse himself, had to go to collect the body. His sister and her children were now destitute, and he had to provide for them. Other than recounting this episode, Keene tells us little of Akutagawa's family life. We know that he had three sons, one of whom became a symphony conductor, another an actor. But Keene gives us another glimpse of Akutagawa in 1927, the year of his death, through the eyes of the novelist Okamoto Kanoko, who lightly fictionalized a meeting with him at a resort hotel in Kamakura. She had met and conversed with him four years earlier, "and now he has come to look like a sick crane—still a majestic bird, but ravaged by illness."

In June of that year, Akutagawa took a lethal dose of veronal. He left several autobiographical works behind, among them perhaps his masterpiece, "Cogwheels." He is in a state bordering on schizophrenia, "finding peculiar significance in certain colors, or in people casually glimpsed in the street," as Keene describes it. Akutagawa hallucinates semitransparent cogwheels that increase in numbers till vision is nearly blotted out. The outside world impinges: he must leave the hotel room where he is writing and go to collect his brother-in-law's body. Realistic conversations alternate with terrifying visions. "It is a nightmare, impossible to summarize, and filled with a terror that mounts until the final cry: 'I lack the strength to write any more . . . Will no one have the goodness to strangle me in my sleep?'"

Akutagawa's suicide, even more than Arishima's—or perhaps in culmination—had a drastic effect on other writers. Some spoke of it as the turning point in their lives; others abandoned their political convictions or were stunned into silence for years. Many doubted the value of literature itself, if such a gifted and successful man chose to die. And the late twenties was a period when very little work of importance was written in Japan.

II

And now we have reached the four novelists with whom we in the West have some familiarity: Tanizaki Junichirō, best known as the author of *The Makioka Sisters*; Kawabata Yasunari, winner of the Nobel Prize in 1968; Dazai Osamu, the first author I've mentioned who was born in this century, and a probable suicide; and of course, Mishima Yukio, world famous for his spectacular death, and more widely translated and internationally known than any Japanese writer.

Tanizaki Junichirō (1886-1965), to those who know him only through *The Makioka Sisters*, either the novel or the recent film, might seem to be a chronicler of the family life of the bourgeoisie, rather along the lines of Thomas Mann or John Galsworthy. However, the bulk of his writings, and his private life, are considerably more bizarre than that would indicate. Not only a foot-fetishist, of a type that would make Krafft-Ebing chortle with delight, but a masochist and something of a coprophiliac as well, Tanizaki inspires Professor Keene to flights of sustained irony, as the following quotations will indicate. Unlike many Japanese literary critics, who refuse to take Tanizaki altogether seriously, deeming him intellectually shallow and preoccupied with trifles, Keene believes that he is a world-class writer, whose reputation can only grow. Not only was he "incapable of writing a boring line," but he created a body of work that will keep the traditional life of Japan alive as long as we have readers—particularly those readers whose chief interest is in the art of literature itself.

Tanizaki's works take up twenty-eight bulky volumes, and these do not include his letters, his poetry, or his two complete translations of *The Tale of Genji*. He also was born in Tokyo, of a weak and habitually unsuccessful father and a beautiful mother whose influence permeated much of his work, and who was for him the ideal of what Japanese womanhood should be. His paternal grandfather was a convert to Russian Orthodox Christianity; Tanizaki said that the portrait of the Virgin on his grandfather's bedroom wall was the basis for his susceptibility to women, "quite distinct from his feminism." "Tanizaki nowhere suggests, however, that he had inherited his father's exceptional fidelity to his wife."

Tanizaki was a child prodigy. His closest school friend remembered that he and Tanizaki discussed Kant and Schopenhauer when they were eleven or twelve years old. His grandfather and his female relatives took him regularly to visit the Kabuki Theater until he was about ten, when the family became too financially straitened to continue this extravagance—but in the meantime he had seen some of the greatest actors of the day. A teacher persuaded his father that the boy must go on to middle school, and so the father reluctantly scraped up the money somehow; Tanizaki has said that this teacher was the most important influence of his life; otherwise he might have wasted his life as a clerk in an office. When he was sixteen he wrote an essay that stunned his classmates with its sophistication, and the way in which he denounced oriental pessimism. "His insistence on joy as an essential element in human life was the first evidence of the hedonist disposition for which he would be famed." He wrote his first story at seventeen, about a boy whose father would not let him continue in school: "Ever since I was a small child I had disliked military men most of all human beings, and businessmen next. Even supposing a man achieves a worldwide reputation . . . can one say that what he does accords with the way fit for human beings if he robs others of their lives or sheds blood with a sword?" This attitude was hardly typical of boys of his age and time.

Tanizaki began but did not finish his first novel in high school, where, like Kafū, he made himself unpopular by boasting of his family and putting down young men who came from the countryside. In Tokyo Imperial University, "he enrolled in the Department of Japanese Literature, always known as a haven for students who chose not to study." Because he had decided to become a writer, he didn't feel it was necessary to study. He began to hang out in the licensed quarters and soon contracted a venereal disease. He had turned out to be a thoroughly unfilial child; but he was able to redeem himself in the eyes of his family when he began to publish, in 1909. His early story, "The Tattooer," sounded themes that were to recur, obsessively, in his writings. The tattooer is first attracted to a girl when he gets a glimpse of her naked foot. "To his sharp eyes a human foot was as expressive as a face . . . This indeed was a foot to be nourished by men's blood, a foot to trample on their bodies." This idea is coupled with the vision of a cruel and beautiful woman. His taste for "the perverse, the sinister, the ingeniously wrought" lasts right through to the end, when he writes, in Diary of a Mad Old Man, that, given equality in beauty, "I would be more susceptible to the woman with a bad character." One wonders about Mother . . .

In The Kylin, Tanizaki draws on historical Chinese sources, but the novel still bears a strong resemblance to his other sado-masochistic tales: Confucius arrives at the court of Duke Ling, who begs the sage to stay and teach his wisdom. Confucius

94

says he would like to stay if the duke truly wishes to foster the happiness of his people. "Before long," says Keene, "he has become so absorbed with the pursuit of virtue that he neglects Nan-tzu," his beautiful consort. When she rebukes him, he replies, "The beauty of your body has always been my greatest strength, but the sage's mind has given me an even greater strength." Keene remarks that "the slavish worship of beautiful women is so frequent a theme in Tanizaki's writings that the duke's assertion that a more powerful force exists in the world is bound to startle anyone familiar with [his] work." Nan-tzu decides to seduce Confucius. "At this point the reader is likely to foresee that Nan-tzu will achieve precisely what she predicts, regardless of what history has to say about the ironclad virtues of Confucius," but he rebuffs her. Then she threatens him with torture: "The loving attention Tanizaki bestows on his descriptions of the maimed and tortured is characteristic of this period of his career . . . ." But the sage remains obdurate. As he departs, Confucius says, "I have never yet met a man who loved virtue as much as he loved sex," which, Keene tells us, is an authentic quote from the Master.

Tanizaki's story, "The Secret," concerns a man who dresses in drag and pretends to be a woman; he is embarrassed when, at the theater, he is recognized by a woman who is not only more fashionably dressed than he, but is also a former mistress. Around this time (1911), Kafū wrote an essay about Tanizaki which stressed three characteristics of his writing: a mysterious depth produced by carnal dread; an intense pleasure in reacting to physical cruelty, and the perfection of his style. This article greatly raised Tanizaki's reputation, and they remained on good terms until Kafū died—although, knowing the character of both men, it is easy to see why they didn't become close friends. Tanizaki's first collection of stories appeared at the end of 1911. One of the stories, "The Devil," describes the actions of a young man who achieved a carnal thrill from licking the snot from the handkerchief of his beloved. This sort of thing got him branded as "Diabolist," and his vivid sexual activities and financial fecklessness—which had him hiding from his creditors—helped color the sobriquet.

In 1914 Tanizaki wrote a novella called *Jōtarō*, which was called his *Picture of Dorian Gray*, but Keene concludes that it "is less a justification of aestheticism or hedonism than a farcical account of the delights of masochism. Jōtarō is a lazy writer who feels that there is nothing in the world worth writing about. His musings on emptiness are interrupted by a young would-be disciple named Shōji. "Shōji naturally takes off his shoes before entering the house, but Jōtarō insists that he also remove his socks; the sight of the young man's naked feet, even though they are not entirely clean, gives [him] a pleasing sensation"—in fact the dirt is affecting; it has a kind of sweetness! When Shōji leaves, Jōtarō regrets that he hasn't been able to corrupt him. Jōtarō dreams of being victimized by a beautiful girl. He has begged women to beat him up and kick him. Alas, he concludes that "the more a woman cared for him, the less likely she was to give him the kind of pleasure he craved. . . . Unfortunately, there was almost no chance of finding a Japanese woman who would behave so cruelly," Keene continues. He finally encounters a prostitute who will fulfill his wishes: She "shows such enthusiasm for her work that soon his body is covered with welts. He all but goes out of his mind with joy." There is more to the story than this, but this will do.

"The Golden Death," a story of a narcissistic young man, is notable despite its many flaws, for Tanizaki's emphasis on the body—"a people which despises the flesh will never produce great art." Mishima Yukio devoted an essay to this work in the last year of his own life. As the protagonist of the story dies in the end, having covered his body with gold leaf (to take part in an orgy) which chokes his pores, Mishima declared that "anyone who attempts to make of himself a work of art will be tempted repeatedly by the desire to commit suicide; to go on living means relinquishing the attainment of beauty. . . ." This has a more than ominous ring to it.

Given the zest with which Tanizaki dwelt on the perversities of men and the cruelty of women, it is not surprising that married life to normal Japanese women presented certain problems. (I see I am picking up Professor Keene's tone.) In his only admittedly confessional novel, *The Sadness of the Rebel*, Tanizaki describes his wife, in the introduction, as a model daughter-in-law, and suggests that he has given up his dissolute life. But not long after writing these words he ordered his wife and child out of the house and sent them to live with his parents. This was to enable him to fool around with his wife's younger sister, Seiko, a cold-blooded and kittenish young woman who was more his type than the perfect wife. Keene says elsewhere that it was perhaps no accident that Tanizaki was always fascinated by cats (in *Landscapes and Portraits*, 1971). Seiko, like Naomi, the heroine of *A Fool's Love* (1925) not only has a name common in both West and East, but possesses un-Japanese features, and an un-Japanese lack of decorum. However, when his friend, the eminent novelist Satō Haruo came to stay and noticed how wretchedly Tanizaki treated his wife—first sympathizing and then falling in love with her—and asked him to give her up, Tanizaki balked. He broke off all relations with his closest friend, and played dog-in-the-manger for five years, until he finally relinquished her. Sad to relate, Satō's own work "noticeably declined in quality after his happy marriage . . . and during the last thirty years of his life he wrote nothing as interesting as his earlier works." Clearly, Japanese men of letters need to be miserably mated in order to succeed.

Meanwhile, Tanizaki's worship of Seiko's feet—"the most beautiful objects in the whole world," he remarked—and his adulation of the West reached its acme in the early 1920's, when he moved to the foreign section of Yokohama and led a totally western-style life.

Then came the great earthquake of 1923. In the same

instant that he felt concern for his family in Yokohama, the epicenter of the earthquake, he felt joy well up inside him: "Tokyo will become a decent place now! . . . Orderly thoroughfares, shiny, newly paved streets, a flood of cars, blocks of flats rising floor on floor . . . and (threading through the city) elevated lines, subways, streetcars. And the excitement at night of a great city, a city with all the amusements of Paris or New York, a city where night life never ends. . . . That is the inevitable trend of the times, and whether one likes it or not, this is what will happen." Perverse in this as in all else, when it happened, Tanizaki did not like it. In 1934 he wrote, "Now that Tokyo has at last become Westernized, I have bit by bit come to dislike the West."

While waiting for Tokyo to be rebuilt, he moved to the Kansai region, partly because he dreaded earthquakes, but mainly because "the old Japan of Osaka, Kyoto, and Nara . . . had conquered me before I knew it."

Keene explains that "the change in Tanizaki was . . . not very different from that which many other Japanese men have experienced in their forties, when they discover as if for the first time the comfort of sitting on tatami and drinking saké with friends. . . ." At any rate, the move to Kansai, and its women whom he admired above all others, inspired his greatest literary period. *Manji* (a word shaped like the Buddhist swastika), *Tade kuu Mushi*, called *Some Prefer Nettles* in its translation, *The Secret History of the Lord of Musashi, Ashikari and Sasameyuki* (*The Makioka Sisters*) poured from his pen, interrupted only by his translation of *The Tale of Genji*, which took two years out of an extremely creative period of his life. However, this was wartime, censorship was severe, and even parts of *Genji* were censored as being disrespectful of the imperial household. During the Pacific War, *The Makioka Sisters* was virtually all that he wrote, and that too was censored by having its publication suspended. In *Landscapes and Portraits*, Keene quotes the notice that appeared in the magazine that had printed the first two installments of the novel:

"Having taken into consideration the possibility that this novel might exert an undesirable influence, in view of the present exigencies . . . of the war, we have regretfully decided from the standpoint of self-discipline to discontinue further publication." The editor had been summoned before a board of army officers to justify the publication of this work. Understandably, he backed down. "*The Makioka Sisters* is by no stretch of the imagination an anti-war novel, but the leisurely pace of its descriptions of pre-war Japan exasperated the militarists, who insisted on a positive, exhortatory literature to suit the heroic temper of the times. Needless to say, it was precisely the relaxed, gossipy atmosphere of *The Makioka Sisters* which most appealed to readers, who were exhausted by the resolute attitudes expressed in other fiction at that time."

When the novel was published, after the Japanese surrender, it was an immediate best seller, won numerous prizes, and its author was invited to dine with the Emperor. The diabolic novelist had become the chronicler of a not-so-remote past: "The book is rather old-fashioned in its narrative method, but Tanizaki created a solid sense of reality . . . He seems intent on preserving for posterity the memory of Japan . . . [in] the mid-1930s, when it was still possible for people of the upper class to lead civilized, even cosmopolitan lives." Who, having read this beguiling novel, can forget the account of the visit to see the cherry blossoms at the Heian shrine, or the account of the firefly hunt (first told to us by Edward Seidensticker in a brief excerpt in *Modern Japanese Literature*)?

The book, though far from being a confessional novel, was based on Tanizaki's life. His third wife, Matsuko (the second hadn't lasted very long, being almost as gentle and compliant as the first) was the model for Sachiko, the principal sister of the novel, and her sisters and daughters are portrayed with reasonable fidelity. As usual, the male characters are pale, flabby creatures; the emphasis was on the women. Interestingly enough, the shy, old fashioned sister—around whom the entire action pivots, as her relatives try to find her a suitable husband—is the one who plays the piano and drinks white wine, while her wilder young sister performs the traditional dances. "The old and the new have become inseparably intertwined, and it is no longer possible to live in a purely Japanese manner."

After another impressive novel, *The Mother of Captain Shigemoto* (1949-1950), Tanizaki retranslated *The Tale of Genji*! Freed of worry about censorship, and with new research by *Genji* scholars in hand, he wanted to re-do it in a more colloquial style. It took him just as long as the first version, partly because his health had begun to fail. But he was far from finished. In 1956 the first installment of *The Key* appeared, and caused a sensation. It described the sexual life of a middle-aged professor and his wife, and his efforts to persuade this ladylike person to indulge him in various excesses which lead to his death. The exploration of character, which had been such an important part of Tanizaki's work, went by the board, in favor of an exclusive preoccupation with middle-aged sex. Although the book was wildly successful, both in Japan and abroad, its importance has probably been overrated. In *The Bridge of Dreams*, he reverts to the old obsessive themes: the protagonist suckles at the breast of his stepmother although he is now eighteen years old. *The Diary of a Mad Old Man* followed, in 1961-62, concerned with love in old age. It is hilarious and satiric, in the tradition of great artists who have ended their careers with comedy. Fifty years after the story in which the narrator licks the soles of a person's feet and sucks at the toes, an old man, kneeling in the shower, takes his daughter-in-law's foot and crams her toes into his mouth.

To save the feelings of the reader, and my own, I have omitted an account of Tanizaki's coprophilia. Keene gives a detailed—perhaps too detailed—account of this obsession in *Landscapes and Portraits*. But perhaps it is appropriate to mention that the last sentence of *The Makioka Sisters* is unique in world literature: "Her diarrhea never did stop that day, and even after she boarded the train it still continued." Unaccountably, the recent film of the book failed to deal with this recurring theme. . . .

Kawabata Yasunari (1899-1972) visited the United States in the early sixties, and spoke and answered questions at the University of Washington, among other places. I asked him if his work (of which I had read *Snow Country, Thousand Cranes,* and a couple of stories) had been influenced by French Symbolism. As my question was translated, Kawabata was visibly upset, and retorted that he had *never* been influenced by any work of Western literature; that the only influence on him had been works of classical Japanese authors. (Some of his anger may have been due to the translator, hastily recruited from the Economics Department, who might have used a word which was closer to imitation than influence.) I have learned, in reading Dr. Keene, that Kawabata habitually repeated this denial, although Keene speaks of the influence of Proust and Joyce more than once, if not of the Symbolists. It is striking that, of all the authors discussed so far, Kawabata is the only one who does not acknowledge having read or benefited from Western thought, other than a passing reference to Dostoievski.

Keene is silent about Kawabata's early education; however he is illuminating on the subject of his early background. Kawabata's parents died when he was a child—his father when he was two, and his mother the following year. He was sent to grandparents, but the grandmother died when he was seven. Two years later his only sister died. The boy and his grandfather were left alone in the world, and as more and more of his kinsmen died, Kawabata was given the nickname "Master of Funerals," a phrase which he used as the title of an early work. So his obsession with death, and his austere and reclusive temperament, become understandable. Kawabata's life with his grandfather was a subject he returned to over and over again, although his "Diary of a Sixteen-Year-Old" was probably written in 1925, the year it was published—or at least heavily edited, as the style, unlike his other juvenile writings, "is free from literary language and conventional flourishes." The love and disgust which the lad feels for the blind and failing old man is portrayed with agonizing clarity and simplicity.

He began publishing in 1921, but his most important story, and the one that brought him fame, was "The Izu Dancer," published in 1926. Depressed after being jilted (by a fifteen-year-old girl), Kawabata went on a walking tour where he encountered a group of traveling players, and this experience, along with his attraction to a young girl of the troupe, is the basis of the story. The narrator considers asking the girl to spend the night with him, "but when by accident he sees her emerge naked from the steam of an outdoor hot spring, he discovers she is still a child, despite her grownup clothes and way of arranging her hair. This discovery, far from disappointing him, frees him of constraint, and he happily accompanies the troupe to Shimoda, where they part." Kawabata's fascination with virgins recurs again and again in his writing. Perhaps, as Mishima suggested in his introduction to the English translation of *The House of the Sleeping Beauties*, Kawabata was fascinated by virginity because it is impossible to take it without losing it, an interpretation that would have fascinated Heisenberg.

Another critic believed that Kawabata's fascination for "the mystic beauty of virginity" could be traced to having been jilted by the fifteen-year-old, but Kawabata was at pains to deny this: " . . . I have a feeling that I have never taken a woman's hand in mine with romantic intentions. . . . And it is not only women I have never taken by the hand—I wonder if it isn't true of life itself as far as I am concerned?"

Kawabata left many books unfinished, including *Crystal Fantasies,* in which he adopted stream-of-consciousness (and did admit to an interviewer years later that he had read

Ulysses both in its Japanese translation and in English), and immensely long paragraphs which may have been influenced by Proust. There are also some admitted debts to Freud in stories of this period.

Kawabata's two finest works are the novels, *Snow Country* (1937) and *Thousand Cranes* (1959)—both translated by Seidensticker, whose translations were certainly an important factor in Kawabata's Nobel Prize. For the average Western reader, *Snow Country* is perhaps what we think of as typically "Japanese": elusive, misty, inconclusive. It begins with these now-famous sentences: "When the train emerged from the long tunnel at the provincial boundary, they were in the snow country. The depths of the night had turned white. The train stopped at a signaling station." Leaving aside any intended Freudian implications of this opening, the passage transfers us to another world, and the breaking of ties to this one: wife, family, city. The narrator hears the voice of a young girl ring out with extraordinary clarity as she calls to the stationmaster, asking him to look out for her sick brother. This is Yōko, the young, fresh girl to whom he is attracted. The other woman in the story is a geisha, Komako, whom he already knows. The triangular relationship is never developed explicitly. The novel ends with a fire. Yōko leaps from the second floor of the burning building, and Komako takes her into her arms. The narrator stands by helplessly, always the bystander.

During the Pacific war, Keene says, "Kawabata attempted to understand the special character of a country for which so many men were dying. He drew examples from the literature of the past . . . to demonstrate that the Heian traditions had survived, despite their apparent weakness." The femininity of *The Tale of Genji* survived the vicissitudes of war better than the strongest castle. However, Kawabata was unable to resist the pressures brought to bear on writers during the war, and joined various official organizations devoted to patriotism and propaganda. Afterwards he wrote,

"And it goes without saying that I was never caught up in a surge of what is called divine possession, to become a fanatical believer or blind worshipper of Japan. I have always grieved for the Japanese with my own grief; that is all. . . . But the defeat actually brought freedom of the spirit and the sense of what it means to live in peace." He went on to say that his postwar life was to consist of "remaining years"— although he was not yet fifty. The master funeral-goer had had to write eulogies for three of his closest friends since the war ended. But the defeat itself had sent him into a profound depression: "I felt like one dead. I felt as if I had been soaked to the bone in the cold, wintry rains and buried in the fallen leaves of my old home, Japan. . . ."

In 1949 Kawabata visited Hiroshima. Later he was criticized for continuing on to Kyoto, to sightsee. He defended himself by saying, "Perhaps Hiroshima and Kyoto are the two extremes of Japan today. I have been examining two such disparate sights at the same time . . . It goes without saying that looking at old objects of art is not a hobby or a diversion. It is a matter of life and death." And indeed, in this period, he began his impressive collection of art.

Thousand Cranes and *The Sound of the Mountain* were published in one volume. As usual, he deprecated his own work in severe terms. The most important character in *Thousand Cranes* is the tea ceremony itself. The story—mainly concerning a woman's love for a man and then for his son—is secondary. And the leading male character, like the protagonist of *Snow Country*, is little more than a peg around which to drape the snowy arms of his women. *The Sound of the Mountain* has the most believable female characters in all of Kawabata's work.

Death, which had preoccupied him throughout the war, was still a central concern: "Never a day went by but I thought of death." Shingo, the elderly protagonist, dreams incessantly of dead friends, and the sound of the mountain itself seems to be a premonition of death. His memory is going, including,

104

near the end, the remembrance of how to tie his necktie. He sees death's approach in the face of his wife. But the novel has a counter-theme: his son is keeping a mistress, and when the son's wife learns of this she decides to abort their child. However, the mistress insists on bearing the son's child, even though they have parted company. Keene comments that almost every remark that the characters make is intuitively interpreted, and "the paragraphs are generally no more than a nervous sentence or two. But Shingo's love for his daughter-in-law, which he becomes aware of through his dreams, and her devotion to an old man hovering on the brink of senility, are conveyed with a warmth rare in Kawabata."

His extraordinary work, *The House of the Sleeping Beauties* (like all his major works, translated by Seidensticker) published in the early sixties, tells of an old man who visits a secret house where old, impotent men lie beside the bodies of young girls, naked and heavily drugged. "The love of the virginal, a familiar theme, is given new poignance here by the fact that the man who lies beside them cannot violate their virginity." The novel, though brief, is beautifully organized, and complete in itself as perhaps no other work of Kawabata's is.

In 1968 he went to Stockholm to accept the Nobel Prize, accompanied by his faithful translator (who had some problems there, being treated as an interpreter rather than the man who had brought Kawabata's work to world-wide attention; for the most part, the novels had been translated from Seidensticker's English rather than from the Japanese; translators have ways of checking on this, as Seidensticker told me; alas, this practice does not include royalties to the original translator, who is ill-paid at best). Kawabata went on from Stockholm to travel in Europe and return to America. He was dreadfully distressed to learn of the suicide of Mishima, whom he had discovered when the latter was a young writer. In April of 1972, less than four years after winning the Nobel Prize, Kawabata went to his office and committed suicide by inhaling gas. He left no note, but his reasons for doing so are perhaps made clear by meditating on his life from the beginning.

The Setting Sun, by Dazai Osamu (1919-1948) was the first modern Japanese novel to be read by Americans, including me, although a short story, "Villon's Wife" appeared in *New Directions 15* (both translated by Donald Keene). I wonder if others who read this novel in 1956 remember as vividly as I do the poem,

> Last Year nothing happened
> The year before nothing happened
> And the year before that nothing happened.

(This was quoted by Dazai as a memory of the war years, in which of course a great deal happened.) And there is a passage which appears when the family in the novel has reached the pit of misery, which has remained with me almost word for word: "I suddenly wondered whether the sensation of happiness might not be something like faintly glittering gold sunken at the bottom of the river of sorrow. The feeling of that strange pale light when once one had exceeded all the bounds of unhappiness. . . ."

And a third quotation, when the novel is nearly at an end: "Victims. Victims of a transitional period of morality. That is what we both certainly are. The revolution must be taking place somewhere, but the old morality persists unchanged in the world around us and lies athwart our way. However much the waves on the surface of the sea may rage, the water at the bottom, far from experiencing a revolution, lies motionless, awake but feigning sleep."

Simply by the accident of memory, these three passages sum up Dazai's life and work as well as a deliberate choice of quotations could do.

Dazai was born in a remote part of Honshu, the tenth child in a wealthy and privileged family, which included about thirty people living under one roof. Dazai's mother, "perhaps exhausted by repeated childbirths, was unable to look after him, and he was left in the care of an aunt whom he supposed for years to be his mother. A feeling that he had been rejected by his mother may account for his unhappy disposition." He did brilliantly in school, although his erratic personal behavior was a portent of what was to come. He tried to kill himself twice before he was twenty. In 1930 he majored in French literature at Tokyo University, although he knew no French and made no effort to learn any. French was a fashionable choice of studies at the time, because many young Japanese found French Symbolism or Surrealism more congenial than English literature, and also because of an attraction to what they knew of *la vie de Bohème* in Paris. Instead of attending any University lectures, Dazai occupied himself with literary and left-wing political matters. He tried suicide again in 1935, leaving behind an envelope containing fourteen stories, entitled *Declining Years*. One story, "Memories", written shortly after one of his suicide attempts, was intended to be his testament to the world.

Dazai's older brother urged him to make a morganatic marriage with a young geisha with whom he had been living for some time, hoping that this would settle him down. This worked fairly well at the beginning, but then Dazai discovered that Hatsuyo, his wife, had had other lovers. Despite his radical politics, Dazai never wavered from the double standard, and "considered a wife's obligation of chastity to be absolute, regardless of the profligacy of her husband." This roused Dazai to thoughts of another attempt at suicide, but instead he decided to write his memoirs; in so doing, he found a reason to go on living. In "Memories", Dazai denied that he had any memories of his parents, only of his aunt, and a maid named Také; she left to get married when he was very young, but he never forgot her, and wrote a touching memoir of her when they met again, thirty years later. Keene says that Dazai "never felt much intimacy with his mother and his few recollections of her are all unpleasant: how she spanked him for wearing his brother's clothes, how she often commented that he was the worst-looking of her many children."

Just before *Declining Years* was published, Dazai wrote: "I sacrificed ten years of my life for this one volume of stories . . . Because of this one book I lost my place in the world, was constantly wounded in my self-esteem and buffeted by the cold winds of the world, and I wandered around in a daze. I squandered tens of thousands of yen. I could not lift my head before my eldest brother, knowing the hardships I was causing him. I burnt my tongue, singed my breast, and deliberately harmed my body beyond any possibility of recovery. I tore up and discarded over a hundred stories. Five thousand sheets of manuscript paper. And all that remained, just barely, was this one volume. Nothing else. The manuscript comes to about 600 pages, but the fee is altogether about sixty yen.

"But I believe in it. I believe that *Declining Years* will take on deeper and deeper colors with the passing years, that it will surely penetrate ever more profoundly into your eyes, your heart. I was born only to write this one volume. From today on I am a corpse through and through. I am merely living out my remaining days." Dazai was twenty-seven years old.

In some ways, "Leaves" may be the most memorable story in the collection; it is a collage of fragments assembled from earlier jottings. It begins: "I was thinking of killing myself. Somebody sent me a bolt of kimono material . . . linen, with a fine gray stripe. No doubt it was meant to be worn in the summer. I decided I would go on living until summer.

"Nora also reconsidered. When she went out . . . slamming the door behind her, she thought, I wonder if I should go back?"

During this period Dazai was not only a Communist, running foolish and irrelevant errands for the Party, as he recalled later, but he was hooked on morphine. Both these addictions seem the outgrowth of his guilt at being rich and well-born, a guilt which surfaced very early, while he was still in high school: "A revolution without a guillotine doesn't make sense. But I did not belong to the lower classes. I was one of those destined to end up on the guillotine. I was a nineteen-year-old high school student, the only member of my class whose school uniform was noticeably well-made. I became increasingly convinced that I was fated to kill myself. I swallowed a good deal of calmotin. It did not kill me"(written in 1946).

Dazai was arrested more than once in the 'thirties; the atmosphere in Japan was tightening up, and growing more repressive in the anticipation of the coming war. At the height of these activities, Dazai once more attempted suicide, this time along with a bar hostess in Kamakura. His family and the police both bore down on him, and as well as being coerced into making promises to behave—all of which he violated, except the vow to remain clear of leftist politics—he also, secretly, committed *tenkō,* but the confession probably came rather easily as at this point he was afraid of the Communist party and its demands. All he wanted to do was write.

Finally the university threw Dazai out; he took an examination to work for a newspaper and flunked that as well. It was then that he tried suicide with the barmaid. His efforts to hang himself ended ignominiously when the rope broke. He gave up, and returned home with a red welt around his neck. His drug addiction became far more serious, and his elder brother bundled him off to a mental hospital where he was confined and kept under surveillance. The diary he kept at this time begins with a series of dates followed by the word "Nothing." He left the hospital cured, but discovered that his wife had been unfaithful with one of his close friends. "As so often when faced with an emotional crisis, Dazai's solution was suicide," Keene remarks. Dazai and his wife planned to take an overdose of barbiturates, but in his words, "I botched my suicide, brilliantly." But this ended his marriage. Soon he

109

met a well-bred schoolteacher whom he married in 1939. Now he wrote some pleasant stories for a change, but "the persona of the devoted, attentive husband and father did not suit the Dazai of fiction."

As he seemed to be running out of material, he next tried adapting works from the West, including what must be a hilarious version of *Hamlet* which one would give a good deal to see performed. Polonius' instructions to Laertes, in slangy Japanese, begin, "First of all, you're not to worry about your school record. If there are fifty in your class fortieth is about the ideal rank. Never, no matter what you do, try to be first. No son of Polonius is apt to be gifted with brains . . . but when you're older and reach a suitably important position, nobody will remember if you cheated. But they won't forget if you fail. . . ."

Dazai went for his army physical in 1941 but, naturally, failed, because of a chest ailment. He was called up several times after that, and trained in attacks with bamboo spears, and then rejected. The few stories he was able to write were censored, or suppressed altogether. However, after the war he defiantly stated that he had been on Japan's side. If Japan had won, Dazai might have felt differently. His most signifi-cant work came after the war, beginning early in 1947 when he wrote "Villon's Wife." Keene's summary of the story, which he translated, goes as follows: "The story opens with a bang as the drunken poet Ōtani bursts into his house late one night . . . he is followed by a man and a woman who run the bar where the husband has been a steady customer since wartime days. They say that Ōtani grabbed a handful of money from the cash register, and they demand that it be returned. . . . His wife . . . agrees to work in the bar as a waitress until she has paid back the stolen money. She comes to enjoy the work, and even though she is struck by a series of disasters—she is even raped by a customer—she manages to remain cheerful, deter-mined to survive." "The success of the story depends less on the plot than on the evocations of the dark days after the war and on Dazai's skill in bringing the work to its existential conclusion, when Satchan reassures her husband, 'There's nothing wrong with being a monster, is there? As long as we can stay alive.'"

Later in the same year Dazai published his extraordinary novel, *The Setting Sun*, the title of which has entered the language to depict an aristocracy whose decline is brought about by the war. The story is mostly told by Kazuko, describing her life with her mother during the war, their move from the family home in Tokyo to a small villa in the country, and the near destitution which follows. Kazuko's younger brother, Naoji, returns from the South Pacific, a nihilist and a no-good. The characters of the brother, the sister and Uehara, an alcoholic novelist, are different aspects of Dazai himself. Dazai, in describing his own family house in Kanagi, compares it to *The Cherry Orchard*. However, the details of the diary kept by Kazuko are borrowed from the diary of an aristocratic young woman, Ōta Shizuko, who had become Dazai's mistress and borne him a child. Ōta Shizuko had intended to use her own diary as material for a novel, but turned it over to Dazai instead—in the tradition of Dorothy Wordsworth and Zelda Fitzgerald, had she but known it. (A comparison between Shizuko's diary and Dazai's version has been discussed, so a footnote informs me, by an eminent Japanese scholar, Donarudo Kin!)

Dazai wonderfully depicts the combination of callousness and hypersensitivity of Naoji/Dazai, particularly in a speech he makes when summoned to the bedside of his dying mother: "'What—another tragic scene? O ye of strong nerves and shallow feelings, have patience and do your duty! We who truly suffer—though indeed the spirit is willing, the flesh is weak—we by no means have the energy to sit with Mama.' He flung on his jacket and went downstairs with me." The last words the Mother speaks are an apology for being a trouble to her daughter. Then she dies, as her daughter says, "the last lady in Japan." The character of Kazuko, who is a dutiful daughter, and tries desperately to hold things together, is unusual in that she pursues the broken-down novelist, Uehara, and insists on bearing his child out of wedlock, after her brother has committed suicide. This is a book of the greatest artistry, including that of its translator.

Dazai's last work was his novel, *No Longer Human*, which Keene calls "the one book Dazai had to write, his final attempt to elucidate himself and his unhappiness. It is an attack on the habits and traditions of Japanese society, but above all it is a record of his alienation from society. Ōba Yōzō . . . is constantly performing for other people in the hopes of ingratiating himself and concealing his true nature." He insists that he is disqualified as a human being, which is true, in that "he was sensitive to insincerity, to the conflicting motives of others, to the dullness of the world and its pleasures . . . Yōzō, far from being nonhuman, carries certain human virtues to intolerable extremes . . . But this is not the whole story about Yōzō. Although he records in his notebooks with devastating honesty his every transgression of the code of conduct imposed by human society, the cowardly acts and moments of abject collapse are only one side of the truth. In a superb epilogue the only objective witness testifies, 'He was an angel,' and we are suddenly made to realize the incompleteness of Yōzō's self-portrait. In the way that most people fail to see their own cruelty, Yōzō had not noticed his gentleness and his capacity for love."

Finally, Dazai was able to bring off a successful love-suicide, having made a kind of peace with his own history, but not of a kind which could abate his continuing pain. I am reminded of a passage in *No Longer Human* which has also stayed with me over the years: "People . . . commonly speak of the 'wound of a guilty conscience.' In my case, the wound appeared of itself when I was an infant, and with the passage of time, far from healing, it has grown only the deeper, until now it has reached the bone. The agonies I have suffered night after night have made for a hell composed of an infinite diversity of tortures, but—though this is a very strange way to put it—the wound has gradually become dearer to me than my own flesh and blood, and I have thought its pain to be the emotion of the wound as it lived, or even its murmur of affection."

Dazai's body was found in the waters of the Tamagawa Reservoir on June 19, 1948—his thirty-ninth birthday.

Mishima Yukio (1925-1970): How difficult it is to write about this man, about whom we know so much—and so little! He gave us a wealth of information about himself in his various writings, yet the mask is firmly attached. Professor Keene has been able—through much pain, one assumes, as he was a close friend (although he nowhere says so)—to maintain an admirable detachment which one hopes to emulate.

Mishima's father was a government official whose ancestors had been peasants. Mishima didn't care to stress this aspect of his background; rather, he preferred to mention the family of his grandmother, which belonged to the samurai class. As a child, he was sent to The Peers School, where he was encouraged by teachers who recognized his remarkable gifts, evident in his large vocabulary and his penchant— common in gifted children—for large words. Early on, he adopted the elaborate language and ornate style which were to remain hallmarks of his work, although he went to some trouble to avoid the subjectivity of Dazai, a writer whom he detested. Instead, he modeled his writing on the lean, masculine style of Mori Ōgai. Ōgai's diction often suggested a translation from the Chinese, and Mishima decided to imitate him in order to curb any tendencies towards the sensitive and poetic, tendencies which he deplored in Dazai. And he abandoned poetry by the time he reached adolescence. Keene says that his poetry, although self-aware, "lacked the concern for other people—or at least for one other person—that lyric poetry requires."

Mishima's first work to be published—when he was sixteen—was intended for the Peers' School literary magazine but his advisor proposed it for a literary magazine he and three colleagues had been editing. The editors went for a holiday at an inn in Izu, and were convinced that they had discovered a genius. However, concerned that such early publication might be neither good for him nor acceptable to his parents, they persuaded him to adopt a pseudonym. "Mishima" was the name of the station where the editors had changed trains for Izu. The magazine, though small, was widely respected in literary circles, and "The Forest in Full Flower" was read throughout Japan.

In 1944, this story along with others was published in book form. It was a peculiar time for such a work to be published; Japan was losing the war, there was a severe paper shortage, and the government favored works of propaganda. Nevertheless, the original printing of 4,000 copies sold out in a week, evidently because the public was sick of war literature, and longed for something as remote from it as could be imagined.

"Although Mishima would one day gain notoriety by his advocacy of military training and the way of the warrior in a Japan committed to peace, he was quite unenthusiastic about the war while it was actually going on," Keene tells us. He took his physical at his grandfather's home rather than near his house in Tokyo, his family evidently thinking that his frail constitution "would stand out in sharp contrast to strapping farmer's sons in the country, and that he would be rejected," which he was. The regiment he would have entered was massacred in the Philippines.

In 1946 he visited Kawabata, carrying the manuscripts of two stories, and the famous writer was much impressed with the work of this twenty-one-year-old, an opinion not shared by most literary men. Three years later he published an admiring essay on Kawabata, and always considered himself a disciple, although the two men differed greatly. Tradition to Kawabata meant "painting, sculpture and pottery of the past, *The Tale of Genji*, the gardens and architecture of the old temples, the religious teachings of the Zen masters. Mishima was almost totally uninterested in any of these, save *The Tale of Genji*. He sought beauty not in the Japanese past but in the West, especially in classical Greece, and probably never once coveted a work of Japanese art," according to Keene.

Mishima's first full-length novel, *The Thieves* (1948), had an introduction by Kawabata. The work was heavily influenced by Raymond Radiguet, the chief difference being that Radiguet's book is a small masterpiece while Mishima's is a first novel, successful neither artistically nor with the public at the time. The epigraphs include quotes from Wilde, Hofmannsthal, Strindberg and Beaudelaire, which gives us an insight not only into his own predilections but into the literary fashions of the late forties.

In 1949, Mishima published *Confessions of a Mask*, his most self-revealing work. This book was successful both with the critics and the public, and though Mishima published more than thirty other works, this remains near the top of the canon. Public acknowledgment of homosexual tendencies was so rare at this period that many critics chose to believe that Mishima wasn't serious. Even when he published the more overtly homosexual novel, *Forbidden Colors* (1952), one critic stated with amusement that he and others were so ignorant of the homosexual world that Mishima could say what he pleased without fear of being challenged! Generally, the homosexual aspects of *Forbidden Colors* are shrugged off in Japan, even today, as part of a young boy's erotic awakening, or they are even interpreted as being symbolic of the "aridity of the post-war world"! Mishima himself went to a good deal of trouble later on to insist that he was also interested in women.

In a note on the novel, Mishima says that "This book is my farewell message to the realm of death in which I have hitherto been living. Writing this book has been for me a suicide in reverse. If the film of a man committing suicide by throwing himself from a cliff is run in reverse, the man will

115

appear to spring up with tremendous vigor from the valley bottom to the cliff and return to life. My attempt in writing this book was to learn the art of recovering life in this fashion.

"Although this is a confession, I have allowed 'lies' to pasture freely in my novel, and when it seemed appropriate I gave them fodder to eat. Filling the stomachs of the lies in this way kept them from molesting the vegetable patches of 'truth.'

"In the same sense, only a mask which has eaten into the flesh, a mask which has put on flesh, can make a confession. The basic nature of a confession is that 'confessions are impossible.'"

Confessions of a Mask tells the story of a young man whose life has been similar to Mishima's, including his family, the Peers' School, and his education at Tokyo University as well as his experiences in wartime. In *Landscapes and Portraits*, Keene says that it does not matter that the novel was misunderstood. "The purpose of a confession is not to elicit sympathy or understanding but to purge oneself of poison. Mishima describes a young man who is not only incapable of sexual relations with a prostitute—this might be ascribed to fastidiousness" (as was the case with Mori Ōgai)—"but of feeling physical desire for the girl he supposes he loves. He is drawn instead to Ōmi, an older classmate of a rough and unintellectual disposition, and at the end of the book his sexual desire is further aroused by a sweating workman he sees in a café." He also expresses his fascination with the idea of wounding and killing the objects of his desire; early in the book the narrator tells how Guido Reni's painting of St. Sebastian caused him to have his first orgasm. "Later he discovered from his readings in psychoanalytic texts that pictures of St. Sebastian were in the first rank of works of art that attract the invert." Mishima never rid himself of this obsession; the photographs taken near the end of his life are of his chained and naked body pierced by arrows. Keene quotes a passage from *Death in Venice*: "Forbearance in the face of fate, beauty constant under torture, are not merely passive. They are a positive achievement, an explicit triumph: and the figure of Sebastian is the most beautiful symbol, if not of art as a whole, yet certainly of the art we speak of here."

Mishima's next important work—to put aside consideration of the popular works he wrote at this time, and continued to write—was *Thirst for Love* (1950), in which he said farewell to the confessional novel. It concerns a widow who becomes her father-in-law's mistress, and is said to have been written under the influence of Mauriac, particularly in its tight dramatic structure. Mishima was learning his craft. After Mauriac, Mishima went on to Racine, who influenced his plays, which he had begun to write in 1948. In 1951, Mishima began to publish *Forbidden Colors*, which is not considered one of his more successful works, although I confess to a fondness for it—as would any woman, I believe—for its extraordinarily empathetic description of childbirth, unique in the writing of men, so far as I know. (The book, which appeared in two parts in Japan, was published here in 1968, in a rather clumsy translation by Alfred Marks.)

In 1951, Mishima began the first of his travels abroad. He was enthralled by Greece, even modern Greece, as one might expect. One speculates that it was exposure to the art of Classical Greece that prompted him, around this time, to take up weight lifting, and to build up his frail scholar's body to the close approximation of an antique torso. Classicism, whether Greek or, increasingly, Japanese, fascinated him more and more, and is evident in the structure of works like *After The Banquet*, the account of an affair between a rather vulgar fifty-year-old woman who owns a restaurant and a prominent aristocratic sixty-year-old politician (1960). *The Sound of Waves* (1954) was inspired by the ancient romance of *Daphnis and Chloë*, changing the characters from shepherd and shepherdess to fisherboy and fishergirl on the Ise coast.

But Mishima had more to say in a contemporary vein. Indeed, *Kinkakuji*, called here *The Temple of the Golden Pavilion* (1956), may be his most nearly perfect work. I am struck by the fact that all of Mishima's major works have the curious effect, not just of imparting ideas to the reader, but of leading the reader to *think*: muse, speculate, even philosophize—as attested by the copious notes in all my copies of his books. This is particularly striking in *The Golden Pavilion*, which turns certain of our assumptions about life upside down, particularly our belief that the highest tribute that can be paid to something beautiful is to preserve it. It is well known that the novel is based on a real event—the destruction of a famous Kyoto temple. We realize from the beginning that Kinkakuji is doomed; the fascination lies in our attempt to understand the motives which prompted its ruin. This too is a classic novel, tightly structured, in which the first chapter introduces the themes which will be developed throughout: Mishima described the style as "Ōgai plus Mann." The ugly young monk, Mizoguchi, whose stammer expresses his alienation and his inability to communicate his thoughts, is described with stringent economy. He has come to live near the temple as an acolyte to beauty, a beauty which comes to dominate him to such an extent that he believes he can have no life so long as it exists. Mizoguchi is unable to make love to a woman because she, poor temporal being, cannot compare to the absolute beauty of Kinkakuji. "If one compared this beauty to a sound, the building was like a little golden bell that has gone on ringing for five and a half centuries. . . . But what if that sound should stop?" Was it really necessary to destroy the building, he wonders, and then recalls a passage from a Zen text which begins, "When ye meet the Buddha, kill the Buddha!"

So he goes ahead, step by methodical step. When the flames rise around him—an intolerably beautiful and painful scene—he runs from the temple and throws away the poison and knife he had brought along in order to commit suicide. "Then I noticed the pack of cigarettes in my other pocket. I took one out and started smoking. I felt like a man who settles down for a smoke after finishing a job of work. I wanted to live."

In 1958, Mishima married the daughter of a well-known painter, and wrote a series of novellas and plays, the novel, *Kyoko's House*, which was a failure, and *After the Banquet*, which certainly wasn't. Although in one aspect *After the Banquet* is a political novel—with the finest account in fiction of a Japanese election—one is apt to acquire an erroneous impression of Mishima's politics, which would seem to be sympathetic to socialism. In fact, Mishima was becoming wrapped up in the martial aspects of Japanese tradition— connected, no doubt, with his own increasing interest in martial sports. He became fascinated with the idea of the infallibility of the emperor, although Keene says that this has been misinterpreted. "For Mishima the emperor was the abstract essence of Japan itself, and only incidentally related to any particular emperor, including the present one." Along with this, Mishima's xenophobia increased. Westerners found themselves increasingly repelled by the parts of his late novels that venomously portray us. However, though these feelings ran deep, they did not prevent Mishima from looking to foreigners for friendship and praise. Like the emperor himself, Japan was an abstraction: "the West he loved was what made up his daily life—the house he lived in, the clothes he wore, the food he ate, the majority of the books he read."

During the seven or eight years following *After the Banquet*, Mishima wrote prolifically, both in the serious and the popular vein; although the serious novels sold well, he depended on the popular works to provide him with the funds necessary to maintain his impressive lifestyle. *The Sailor who Fell from Grace with the Sea* (1962) was a minor work, later made into an American movie, which involved a group of boys who determine to kill the sailor in question. But even as Mishima wrote this and other works, he was planning a major tetralogy which would be called *The Sea of Fertility*. The entire work, which commenced with *Spring Snow* (1969), is the story of four people, each born with the same birthmark. Honda, a man who knows all of them, believes he is able to recognize in each the reincarnation of the same being. Keene summarizes as follows: "Honda is the classmate of the first manifestation of this being, Matsugae Kiyoaki, a boy of extraordinary beauty who belongs to an upper-class family. He is spoiled and willful, and hates doing what people expect of him. For this reason he professes indifference when he is informed that Satoko, the girl to whom he has long been attracted, is about to be engaged to a prince." However, the announcement of this engagement stimulates his ardor, and he persuades Satoko to meet him secretly, although he realizes how dangerous this is. Satoko becomes a nun, and Kiyoaki, though ill, goes to visit her at the convent in Nara, repeatedly begging for one more glimpse of her, which is denied. He dies, telling Honda that they will meet again under a waterfall.

Spring Snow is beautifully written, essentially lyric, as if the tight rein under which Mishima had kept himself had suddenly given way. The aristocratic world just after the first decade of the century has ended is brilliantly evoked. Like Akutagawa, Mishima was fascinated by the aristocrats who built Victorian mansions with billiard rooms, wine cellars and cut glass chandeliers, but he also described the Japanese aspects of their lives: the gardens, the kimonos, the elaborate etiquette.

Runaway Horses (1969), the second volume, takes place about twenty years later. Honda is now a promising young judge who attends a *kendō* exhibition near Nara, where he notices a young and talented fencer; later he sees the lad bathing under a waterfall. Under the boy's arm is the birthmark, which reminds Honda of Kiyoaki's prediction. But Isao isn't at all like Kiyoaki, either in his looks or his aspirations. He longs to regenerate the spiritual side of Japan, and intends to begin by ridding the emperor of his corrupt advisers. He and his friends plot to blow up the Bank of Japan as well, but they are betrayed and Isao is arrested. Honda resigns from the bench to defend him, and Isao is given a light sentence. But when he is released from prison "he goes to kill one of the prime targets on the conspirator's list, then commits *seppuku* while gazing into the rising sun."

The Temple of Dawn followed a year later. Now the reincarnation of Kiyoaki is a Thai princess. "As a small girl she baffles everyone by insisting that she is really Japanese. When Honda asks her questions about Kiyoaki and Isao she answers correctly, without hesitation. Honda next sees her nine or ten years later, in Japan. By now she has forgotten about her previous lives and does not even remember her meeting with Honda when she was a child." The climax of this volume—perhaps of the whole series—describes the ritual slaughter of a goat during a Calcutta festival, and the burial ghats of Benares which suggest the endless cycle of birth, death and rebirth. The second half of the book is set in postwar Japan, and deals with the corruption of the aristocracy, in which the influx of foreigners plays a contributing part. The two halves of the book don't really fit together. The end of this volume seems an echo of Proust, when Honda, who had hoped to be her lover, peeps through a hole into a room where the Thai princess is making passionate love with a Japanese countess. She too dies young, bitten by a cobra in her garden.

The fourth volume, called in English *The Decay of the Angel* (1970), curiously enough casts doubt on the entire elaborate enterprise. The last incarnation of Kiyoaki is Toru, a young workman. Honda, old now, catches sight of him, lightly dressed because it is summer, and notices the birthmark. He adopts Toru, educates him, and has him taught how to behave. Toru is a clever pupil but shows no trace of gratitude. He is calculating and deceitful, taking "special pleasure in betraying others after having once gained their confidence, and in humiliating Honda, even molesting him physically." The former lover of the Thai princess shows up and, after testing Toru, announces that he is a fake; far from dying at twenty, like the others, he is no doubt destined to live a long time. After hearing this, Toru takes poison which does not kill but blinds him. At the end, "the flowers about him are withered; he perspires freely; his unwashed body gives off a foul odor . . . He is tended by a crazy woman who is soon to bear his child." So Toru was a false reincarnation. Or was he? "Perhaps Mishima intended for us to realize that the semidivine being we have seen for the fourth time has now lost his magic and will dissolve into common clay."

In the last scene of the novel, Satoko the nun, now ancient but still beautiful, receives the aged Honda. She politely insists that she has never heard of Kiyoaki, and suggests that he was a figment of Honda's imagination. The last words of the novel describe the convent garden: "There was no other sound. The garden was empty. He had come, thought Honda, to a place that had no memories, nothing. The noontide sun of summer flowed over the still garden."

As Keene informs us in *Landscapes and Portraits*, Mishima repeatedly told his friends that when he finished *The Sea of Fertility* there was nothing left for him but to kill himself. Mishima told Keene in August of 1970 that he had written the ending of the work "in one breath." The last volume is shorter than the others, and shows marks of haste. Mishima had chosen November 25, 1970 as the date of his death—a date he inscribed on the last page of the manuscript.

So many people have speculated on Mishima's ending that I am not going to add one word more. Because of the spectacular nature of his last days, and his ritual death, it is hard to be objective about the lasting importance of his work; those events cast a shadow that has not yet passed away.

With his account of the death of Mishima, Donald Keene ends this massive work—from which I have lightly sketched a few portraits among the many he has discussed, and on which I have heavily leaned, without attempting to cover the many schools and influences so thoroughly elucidated in over a thousand pages. I hope that this account of brilliant eccentrics and major writers will encourage some of you to read this book for yourselves, and to search out some of the works here mentioned; or to go back, as I have done, to the books translated over the past quarter of a century, to feast on their riches and meditate on their profundities. We need to know these Japanese—in as much as we are able to comprehend them—as we have embraced Ibsen, Tolstoy, Proust and Joyce.

Donald Keene's Works: A Selection

The Battles of Coxinga (1951)

The Japanese Discovery of Europe (1952, revised in 1969)

Japanese Literature: An Introduction for the Western Reader (1953)

Living Japan (1959)

Bunraku: The Art of the Japanese Puppet Theatre (1965)

Nōh: The Classical Theatre of Japan (1966)

Landscapes and Portraits (1971, reprinted in 1981 as *Appreciations of Japanese Culture*)

World Within Walls: Japanese Literature of the Pre-Modern Era, 1600-1867 (1976)

Dawn to the West: Japanese Literature of the Modern Era (Volumes I and II) (1984)

Some Japanese Portraits (1978)

The Pleasures of Japanese Literature (1988)

Travelers of a Hundred Ages: The Japanese as Revealed Through 1,000 Years of Diaries (1989)

Seeds in the Heart: Japanese Literature from Earliest Times to the Late Sixteenth Century (1993)

On Familiar Terms: A Journey Across Cultures (1994)

Modern Japanese Diaries (1995)

Translations

The Setting Sun (by Dazai Osamu) (1956)

No Longer Human (by Dazai Osamu) (1958)

Five Modern Nō Plays (by Mishima Yukio) (1957)

Major Plays of Chikamatsu (1961)

The Old Women, the Wife, and the Archer (by Fukasawa Shichirō, Uno Chiyo, and Ishikawa Jun) (1961)

After the Banquet (by Mishima Yukio) (1963)

Essays in Idleness (by Kenkō Yoshida) (1967)

Chushinqura (by Izumo Takeda, Shōraku Miyoshi, and Sōsuke Namiki) (1971)

Madame de Sade (by Mishima Yukio) (1967)

Friends (by Abe Kobo) (1959)

Twenty Plays of the Nōh Theatre (edited and translated) (1970)

The Man Who Turned into a Stick (by Abe Kobo) (1975)

Three Plays by Abe Kobo (1993)

Anthologies

Anthology of Japanese Literature (1955)

Modern Japanese Literature (1956)

NOTE: Japanese personal names are given throughout this book in the traditional Japanese form, that is, with the family name first.

Japanese Family Saga:
Kita Morio

T he chief reason for reading *The House of Nire* is to become acquainted with Nire Kiichiro, founder and inventor of the house and its name. Kiichiro is an unforgettable character all right. Horrible, absurd and powerfully compelling, he sticks in the mind in the way that Sam Pollit, the father in Christina Stead's masterpiece, *The Man Who Loved Children,* won't go away, even as the more admirable characters fade into anonymity.

Kiichiro, offspring of peasants, has abandoned their name for one of his own invention. Having started as an ordinary general practitioner, he studied mental illnesses in Germany, and returned to establish a hospital dealing with mental disorders. Once these facts are established, early in the novel, the reader begins to lick his or her chops: we are happily in the genre of *The Magic Mountain, Ship of Fools,* or even *Grand Hotel,* and settle back for a good read. But, curiously enough, the mental hospital barely figures in the novel. One wonders why the author sets the book in such a milieu without taking advantage of it.

But perhaps the author is correct in feeling that egomania is more interesting than mania, and certainly it is more rife with comic possibility. However, he makes the strategic mistake of killing off Kiichiro on page 246, and the heart goes out of the novel, as well as most of the comedy. We are left with a bunch of characters just as unpleasant in their various ways as Kiichiro without being as interesting. Tetsukichi, Kiichiro's son-in-law, begins to stir our sympathies—put upon as he is by his harridan wife—but his total indifference to his children, his emerging anti-Semitism, and admiration for Hitler's Germany, put an end to that. A hopelessly morose character, Tetsukichi is working, throughout most of the novel, on a history of psychiatry. Perhaps the most interesting aspect of Kita's novel is the careful attention he gives to Japanese prejudices and opinions from the end of the First World War to the end of the Second. So we are painlessly fed a good deal of hitherto unfamiliar information. For example, in telling us about Tetsukichi's history of psychiatry, Kita says, "Despite the fact that Sigmund Freud was clearly the most famous medical man of his age, in Germany his ideas had been subjected to vilification and ostracism for years. Since the medical world in Japan was little more than an off-shoot of the one in Germany . . . Tetsukichi too had never had the least inclination to take his psychoanalytic theories seriously" in 1939.

However, Tetsukichi is not a fool. He realizes that his work, like himself, is simply ordinary, "an aspect of the trivial everyday." It aroused no sense "of something taking shape, of something cold and pure and hard within him," but was merely the product of his obstinate determination.

There is a wonderful passage when Tetsukichi finally finishes his book and sits vacantly at his desk for awhile. Then he goes out for some air and runs into a woman patient. As he is about to speak to her, "she suddenly burst out laughing. The laughter was not only totally unexpected, but possessed all those peculiarities one finds in the laughter of such patients: vacant, moronic, with no rise or fall, no heights or depths, a laughter that made nonsense of any human attempt to understand it." As he turned away from her, towards home, "shoulders hunched, there was something awkward and ungainly about him, the impression of a man trying perhaps to escape from something."

126

There are other beautifully handled episodes, particularly the death of Kiichiro. He is out in a meadow with an assistant, measuring the site of a new hospital (the earlier one having been destroyed in the great earthquake of 1923), and here, near the end of him, we begin to feel some sympathy for this vain, pushing, brash, narcissistic fellow: "'It's all slant lines around here,' said Kiichiro, a little old man whose shoes were covered in mud and who kept wiping the sweat from his forehead, but who showed no obvious signs of fatigue. 'It's no good measuring a place like this just up and down and across, you know. You need your diagonals and perpendiculars on a job like this' . . . . The sky remained a brilliant blue. The larks still sang. The sun beat down now, inducing sleep. The expanse of corn seemed to be caught in a great silence. Some way off the figures of two or three farmers could be seen, but there was no sign of anything else moving. In this peaceful landscape, the little old man and his tall assistant worked endlessly, stretching their long piece of string, walking, stopping, returning, writing their measurements on a piece of paper. . . . Some distance away he [the assistant] could see the small figure of the Director squatting down on the pathway between the cornfields, no doubt making some eager calculations on the drawing paper. But after he had taken a few more paces, he noticed that Kiichiro was leaning forward in a peculiar way, with his forehead apparently touching the ground, like a toad with its head beaten flat by something." Kiichiro, monstrously inflated until this scene by his powerful drives, his inordinate ego, has shrunk and shrunk, to a little old man, to a small figure, to the image of a toad. And now he is dead, in the golden field.

There is another lovely scene, where Tetsukichi's children go to a summer cottage built by their grandfather long ago, dragging their heavy luggage up a steep path to the hot spring, where "the clear-toned cicadas were singing in chorus from the dark cedar woods that lined the roadside. . . . The cottage had been very modern when it was first built, but the damp of the mountains had taken a swift toll on it and now it looked decayed and old. From the side of the veranda, with its glass sliding doors where the putty had come off in a number of places, a partially enclosed walkway led across to the bathhouse where a constant spring of sulfurous hot water bubbled noisily. The children bathed a number of times each day, prancing about in the murky water and splashing it over each other. The hand towels, which had been white when they arrived, gradually changed color, becoming a dull yellow by the time their stay came to an end." That description seems to me to exemplify the Japanese sensibility, with its attention to the subtle attritions of daily life, and the small, vivid signs that indicate the seasons and their passing.

Such eminences as Mishima Yukio and Edward Seidensticker have billed *The House of Nire* as a humorous work. Perhaps humor, rather than poetry, is what is lost in translation. But, with the exception of the first 250 pages, I don't think so. It is a family chronicle of an unlovable tribe, set in a fascinating period, with some fine set pieces. The publisher promises a sequel. One will read it for the author's insights into his society rather than for any curiosity about his dismal characters. As one sees from the quoted passages, it is ably translated by Dennis Keene, except for some sentences that seem to indicate haste on his part. As usual Kodansha has given us a beautifully produced volume and a handsome cover, which puts most of the products of our domestic publishing houses to shame.

The House of Nire, by Morio Kita, translated by Dennis Keene. Tokyo and New York, Kodansha International, 1984.

Section VI

MEN
IN
SPACE

How He Saved His Skin: John Jewitt

H ere is a book of almost universal fascination, embodying as it does a classic tale of adventure, captivity, ingenuity and escape—and all of it true, given a few embellishments by John R. Jewitt's ghostwriter, one Richard Alsop. It's an ideal present for any 12-year-old or any of his or her elders who relished the tales of Stevenson or the story of Robinson Crusoe, a figure that the real-life Jewitt resembles in striking ways.

This narrative is based on a journal that Jewitt kept surreptitiously for two years, after being captured by a Northwest Indian tribe from aboard the brigantine *Boston* in 1803. Maquinna, chief of a Yuquot village on Vancouver Island that was misnamed Nootka by the seafarers and traders who landed there—a name that has persisted to this day—was a remarkable man whose people had suffered much at their hands. In general, the Indians graciously welcomed such visitors, who returned their hospitality by stealing their sea otter furs, the pelts then selling in China for up to $120 each, a great sum at that time. (One trader had collected 6,000 pelts on a single voyage; a total of 48,000 skins had sold for almost $1,500,000.)

The captain of another vessel, the *Sea Otter*, in revenge for the theft of a chisel, had fired his cannon into canoeloads of people alongside his boat, murdering over twenty men, women and children, among them a number of chiefs. Villages had been burned, skins taken from the Indians by force; and casual murders had been committed for little or no reason. As Jewitt himself remarks in his journal, nothing was more sacred to these Indians than the principle of revenge, no people bore insults with less patience, and they would "wreak their vengeance upon the first vessel or boat's crew that offers, making the innocent too frequently suffer for the wrongs of the guilty."

Thus, when the *Boston*, whose voyage began in the English port of Hull in 1802 and came around the Horn with the nineteen-year-old Jewitt on board as ship's armorer, landed in Nootka Sound, Maquinna had a store of grievances. Undoubtedly Capt. John Salter precipitated the slaughter that followed by calling the chief a liar. He had presented Maquinna with a fowling piece, which the chief returned to him, saying that the gun was *peshak*, or bad. The captain threw the weapon to Jewitt to mend while uttering a stream of insults. "Maquinna knew a number of English words, and unfortunately understood but too well the meaning of the reproachful terms that the Captain addressed to him."

The next day the Indians attacked the ship in force, and proceeded to slaughter every man on board with the exception of Jewitt, whose skills as a weapons maker had been noted by the chief, and a sailmaker named Thompson, who was hiding below. Jewitt's account of his behavior when he was taken to Maquinna's house afterward is a striking indication of his character and personality. Maquinna's young son came up to him, and "I caressed him; he returned my attentions with much apparent pleasure, and considering this as a fortunate opportunity to gain the good will of the father, I took the child on my knee, and cutting the metal buttons from off the coat I had on, I tied them around his neck. At this he was highly delighted, and became so much attached to me that he would not quit me."

At midnight the sailmaker Thompson was discovered still

aboard the ship. Jewitt, resourceful as ever, told the chief that Thompson, a man of about forty, was his father. So at dawn, leading Maquinna's young son by the hand, Jewitt went down to the beach and, appealing to the love of father for son and son for father, persuaded the chief to spare Thompson's life. "What a consolation . . . what a happiness would it prove to me in my forlorn state among these heathen, to have a Christian . . . for a companion."

Thompson was a very different character from Jewitt. He might be said to represent the old model of the western adventurer and aggressor. He despised the "savages" to a man, and wished that he could "destroy the whole of the cursed race." He adamantly refused to learn the tribal language, with which Jewitt familiarized himself as soon as possible, and he made no effort to curb his violent temper even at serious risk to his life. But Jewitt says that "I had determined from the first of my capture to adopt a conciliating conduct towards [the Indians], and conform myself . . . to their customs and mode of thinking." In Jewitt we see the emergence of the new model: the compromiser, the arbitrator, one who simulates a concern or affection that he does not feel—in short, a modern man.

I've referred to Jewitt's Crusoe-like aspects. When the Indians were dismantling the *Boston* and carting away the sails and rigging, the muskets, ammunition and cloth, John Jewitt was securing the accounts and papers of the ship, the captain's writing desk with its writing implements and an account book in which he was to keep his journal. He also found a volume of sermons, a Bible, and a Book of Common Prayer—items with which he conducted secret Sunday services with Thompson as often as it was possible. He also garnered a collection of tools, which he put to good use in making weapons for the Indians as well as ornaments for the chief and his son, thereby further cementing their friendly feelings toward him.

Throughout the narrative, Jewitt gives a good and largely

accurate description of the various Indian tribes on Vancouver Island—their apparel, methods of hunting and fishing, making war and giving parties. Understandably, he doesn't have the faintest comprehension of the spiritual life of the tribes, their shamans, their veneration of ancestors and the land that they occupy. When, at last, rescue is at hand, Jewitt has no hesitation in lying to his old friend and master, Maquinna, in order to effect his escape, although he does persuade the captain of the brig *Lydia* not to kill the chief.

As might be expected, Thompson comes to a bad end not long after they are freed and on their long way home. Jewitt, on the other hand, takes to the road with copies of his published memoirs, hawking them up and down the eastern seaboard, and even appearing as star in a dramatization of his adventures. Happily ever after, you might say, although he died at thirty-seven, possibly of an old head injury sustained during his capture.

The Adventures and Sufferings of John R. Jewitt, Captive of Maquinna is a handsome volume, carefully annotated and lavishly illustrated by Hilary Stewart, who has written extensively on Northwest Indians. Anyone who receives it as a gift will likely move it from the coffee table to the bedside table.

The Adventures and Sufferings of John R. Jewitt, Captive of Maquinna, illustrated by Hilary Stewart. University of Washington Press, 1987.

The Man Nobody Knew:
Paul Scott

I n the late 'fifties and early 'sixties I spent a fair amount of time in London. This was a period of literary ferment and change—change which, as so often happens, seems permanent and isn't. Kingsley Amis' *Lucky Jim* was causing a stir, and so in lesser degree was *Hurry On Down* by John Wain, followed a bit later by *Room at the Top* by John Braine. People were talking about the poetry of The Movement, particularly of Philip Larkin's dry, skilled, quietly mordant verse. People were going in droves to see "Look Back in Anger" by John Osborne, and then his "The Entertainer," works which savaged the Establishment, as we began to call it, and the class system in particular.

Exciting times. Since they were over I haven't been back. But I've kept up with some of the writers who were my friends in London then. The other day I asked one of them, "Did you know Paul Scott in those days?" He and Scott were exact contemporaries.

"Who?" he replied.

I inquired of another friend if he recalled encountering the author of "The Raj Quartet." He said he vaguely remembered a dim little man smoking a pipe in the back room of a London publishing house. "Drank a lot, didn't he?" No one remembered him from the parties given by a friendly officer of the American Embassy crowded with thirsty literati imbibing her endless supply of Scotch.

Who indeed was Paul Scott? And where was Paul Scott? Hillary Spurling has done her best to explain, in her wise and dispassionate biography. She has woven pieces of reminiscence, letters and conversations with his friends, clients and family into a seamless story, all the more remarkable considering the huge amount of information she was given. Even so, through no fault of hers, we may never know the real Paul Scott, any more than Paul Scott knew himself.

Scott was born in 1920 in the London suburb of Southgate, into a family of artists on his father's side, and of a mother who had written a number of unpublished novels which she burnt on the night before her wedding to Paul's father. Frances Scott came from a working-class background, and was thought to have "married up" when she captured Tom's father, sixteen years her senior. She was, according to Paul, a prime fantasist, whose embroideries on her past became more elaborate with each passing year. For example, she elevated her father, a respectable paperhanger at the time of her birth, to the quite imaginary deanship of a university.

Both to conceal her background and free her fantasies, she severed all relations with her own family when she married. She was ferociously ambitious for her son, whom she saw as a prodigy from birth, claiming he walked and talked before he was one. Scott always insisted that he had had a perfectly ordinary childhood, this in the face of a termagant mother and a father who absented himself, physically and mentally, from his family problems, going to his studio "to paint snow," as Scott described a character in one of his early novels, clearly modelled on his father.

Not the least of Ms. Spurling's virtues as a biographer is the way in which she reveals how obsessively Scott modelled people in his novels after himself and his relatives: the passive father, the domineering mother, the son, like George Spruce in *The Bender*, who was "taught early to think of himself as a gentleman and never to admit to working-class origins. It took him a long time to come to terms with this inbred self-contempt, and longer still to see what a boon his sense of alienation had been to him as a writer." He remained an outsider all his life. When, later, he became obsessed with India, he probably felt more at home there than at home, but still it is his detachment, combined with his sympathy, which makes the novels of "The Raj Quartet" the works of art that they are.

Paul had to leave school when he was fourteen, with his family in straitened circumstances, and no help offered from his father's prosperous relatives. This "demolished all the imaginary futures he had, however vaguely, constructed for himself," based on the artistic pretentions of his family. Instead, he was to be an accountant. Later, Scott would sympathetically remark of another writer with a similar background, "having to become a wage earner at such a tender age may be compared to the effect on Dickens of finding himself at the blacking factory."

Ms. Spurling points out that boys prematurely removed from school, "or otherwise cheated of a future they had taken for granted, form a common pattern in Paul's early fiction. . . . But the one whose loss is most poignant, grave and irreversible is Harry Coomer, or Hari Kumar, in *The Jewel in the Crown*." This harshly truncated education, which no sensitive person ever really recovers from, reinforced Scott's lifelong feeling of being a displaced person. "For the next twenty-five years, the seedy area around Regent Street and Picadilly Circus would remain Paul's familiar London beat" except for the time of war—and India.

After three years' training in England, Paul arrived in Bombay in the summer of 1945. "Like most of his fellows . . . Paul knew virtually nothing about India, hadn't wanted to go there, and was not initially impressed by what he found. . . . People like Paul (who did not care for Kipling, and had not yet read *A Passage to India*) could never understand why they should not treat the Indians as equals, nor why it was axiomatic that Indians could not be allowed to govern themselves."

By early 1944, with ferocious fighting going on in Russia and Europe, Paul had finally been made an officer and was absorbed into the "immemorially trivial Anglo-Indian social round of amateur dramatics, garden parties, tennis, or bridge at the club. . . ." Paul's enjoyment was mixed with exasperation, appalled by "a society so hidebound and ingrown that it treated the imminent collapse of Western Civilization as an unwarranted intrusion on its own comfort."

For the first time, Paul began to drink heavily, having known abstemious days at home with literary friends, "when all any of them needed for intoxication was a mixture of lime juice and sprung rhythm." Perhaps this was bound to happen in any case, but for Paul's personal life, and in part for his writing, the results would be disastrous. Six months later, Paul joined his air supply unit at Imphal. He enjoyed sorting out accounts, drawing up schedules and filling orders. These mundane tasks were backing up the 14th Army's attack on the Japanese near Mandalay. While his fellow novelist-to-be, John Masters, "was battling his way with the 4th Gurkhas up through the tunnels, fortified temples and covered stairways inside Mandalay Hill" in hand-to-hand combat, Paul was loading Dakotas with 88 mm. shells for battering the city. Mandalay was recaptured, Rangoon fell, and by the following August Paul was in Bombay, waiting to be shipped out, when news arrived of the atom bombs and Japan's unconditional surrender.

After mopping-up operations in Malaya, Paul returned to an Indian transit camp where he sat for four months "in love with it all," while his companions chafed at the bureaucratic delays. His troopship left Bombay in May of 1946. Everything of value that Paul was to write, in novel after novel, would draw on this experience of India, and two brief return trips in later years, but his readers tended to assume that "he had been born in India, brought up in a princely state" and had firsthand experience of the political scene and the Indian Civil Service.

Paul returned to a wife, Penny, whom he had wooed and won in a hurry, after a homoerotic episode which had nearly put paid to his army career; and to a miserable England, with horrendous bomb damage, severe rationing, and general exhaustion. Jobs and housing were virtually unobtainable for the millions of discharged veterans. Penny had found a tiny house, and after a depressing round of job-hunting, Paul was taken on as book-keeper by two combined publishing houses, Janus Press and Grey Walls Press. The place was almost entirely staffed by poets, which one of its authors called a thoroughly practical arrangement, given the startling inefficiency of so many publishing concerns run by non-poets. Paul was rapidly promoted to company secretary.

Paul's own poetry was so heavily indebted to Eliot that it read like parody ("Then we consider nothing / or considering nothing can / be nothing to us forever," etc. etc.). He also attempted to write plays, with scant success. The two-headed publishing house collapsed in 1950, and Paul became a literary agent. One can imagine the frustrations of guiding others to the literary success that kept eluding him. His first novel was rejected by seventeen publishers in 1950. By all accounts, he was an excellent agent. As one client put it, "He was good-tempered, smiling, efficient. He replied the following morning. He wrote sense. He read your letters before he answered them."

Sadly, the unfailing kindness and consideration which he showed to his clients and friends was not shared by his own family. By this time Penny had given birth to two little girls, a year apart. Paul's mother, whose husband was now completely deaf, as he had always been deaf to his family's needs, now focussed her formidable energies on harassing Penny. Paul was unable to protect Penny from his mother's bullying, and withdrew more and more into himself, devoting the meager time which was not devoured by his demanding authors to writing novels himself.

Ms. Spurling sensitively analyzes Paul's problems as a writer and the confusions and obscurities of his novels which came from his inability to face his own divided nature. Paul was suffering from amoebiasis which he had contracted in India, a condition which produced "lassitude, apathy, stomach trouble, intermittent fever and depression," which would not be properly diagnosed and treated until the mid-sixties. Paul's iron will fought with these symptoms and rode them down, at terrible cost. He was also sternly repressing his homosexual tendencies, and seems to have done so for the rest of his life. As Ms. Spurling puts it, "homosexuality was also a condition, untreatable and incurable, for all practical purposes impossible to recognise openly. . . . Paul taught himself to ignore what could not be diagnosed."

In 1958 his parents were evicted from their home; the shock was too much for Paul's father, who quietly died, and the formidable Frances came to live with the younger Scotts. "She latched on to us children," said Sally, now aged ten. "It was a kind of taking over. There was no sense of her playing with us. There was a thwarting going on, a spoiling. It was a snatching of us from my mother." Penny's gentleness, her passivity, drove Frances to ever more outrageous provocation. When Penny wrote a novel, and had it accepted that fall, it was more than Frances could bear. Paul came home from the office to face a scene which, for once, forced him to act. He threw his mother out of the house.

Paul's mother appears in a number of his books in various guises, and an unpublished manuscript draft reveals that he believed her maternal feelings were incestuous. Part of his drive and discipline, always, was not only to deny his illness and his homoeroticism, but to deny the romantic and fabulist instincts in himself which reminded him of his mother.

One week after his fortieth birthday, in 1960, Paul quit as an agent to devote himself full-time to writing. He had published five novels, none of them a commercial success, and none of them living up to his or his friend's expectations. It was a daring move, born of desperation. His family was at first delighted, thinking that they might have more of his attention, but this was not to be. Paul, trying to stave off panic about finances, drove himself harder and harder. This led to attacks of self-hate, and ever heavier drinking bouts, from which he emerged with no memory of what had taken place. During one of them he slashed the portrait of himself which had been painted in Kashmir in 1944. It hung forever afterwards in his study, with its throat slit.

Three years later, after three more books, Paul decided to return to India. Many of his advisers felt it was time to drop the subject of India; no one was interested in probing the decline and fall of the Raj. It was supposed to be the preserve of romantic or adventure novels, like those of John Masters— and anyway, Forster had said the last word on India long ago. In January of 1964, Paul went back to Bombay, to meet Indians, to avoid the British remarks, to look around. Ms. Spurling's account of his Indian hosts—or more accurately, hostesses—is enthralling, because her sources are still living, and vivid and generous in their descriptions. We are introduced to the persons who are aspects or personifications of the characters in "The Raj Quartet."

(At this point, television viewers should be reminded that "The Jewel in the Crown" is used as the title for the "The Raj Quartet" when it is the title of the first volume of the series. Also it needs to be said that the version produced by the B.B.C. is more concerned with the British in India. Paul Scott is far more even-handed, indeed intent on giving the Indians scrupulous attention.)

At last for Paul it is all coming together. When he returns to England, he re-reads A Passage to India and is astonished not only by how little English attitudes had changed, but by the novel's powerful prophetic quality. When Nehru dies, and war breaks out between India and Pakistan, Paul, who has just finished writing *The Jewel and the Crown,* says that no one has yet traced these violent divisions "back to the failure of the British government to consolidate and unify. No one has yet had the courage to say that 'Divide and Rule' has come full circle."

Ms. Spurling says that with *The Jewel in the Crown,* Paul's ninth novel, there is "an unmistakable change in the texture of the writing itself: what was weak, bland, pallid, derivative and defensively clenched becomes robust, lucid and open with a strongly individual flavor. It is as if a cloud, the indefinable debilitating self-indulgent invalid sensibility . . . had given way to clear sky."

Paul finished "The Raj Quartet" on his fifty-fourth birthday. Most critics found it to be "a respectable piece of work . . . not worth attention at any great length from front-rank reviewers." Depressed by its reception, Paul went off to lecture in America. He didn't even consider taking Penny with him.

Unfortunately, the habits of will and concentration developed while he was ill, which involved blocking all outside influences, especially the needs of his family, still persisted. Although he had repeatedly stated that Penny was the only woman in his life, and although he wrote her every day that he was away from her, professing his deep need of her, when they were together he could look at her with blank unrecognition. Worse, she felt that sometimes he regarded her with real hatred. Finally Penny reached the breaking point and walked out and—although she had had an emergency bag packed for twelve years—she left with only her purse and went to a women's shelter.

Paul was beside himself. He knew that his inability to express himself—another reaction to his mother's violent outbursts—was to blame as well as his rigid absorption in his writing. But even so, all he could bring himself to write to his daughters was, "I just want her to come back . . . if only temporarily, with no fuss or grand scene, which I simply can't cope with, but as if she's been out shopping or something." But Penny remained in hiding, afraid to speak to him or reveal where she was.

And Paul had to return to America, to teach in Tulsa. On his second year of teaching there he looked so ill that he was persuaded to have a check-up, where cirrhosis of the liver, not unexpectedly, was diagnosed. Paul told his doctor that for years he had drunk a quart of vodka a day and smoked sixty to eighty cigarettes. When cancerous cells were discovered, his daughter Carol came over to take care of him. Then at virtually the last moment Paul's last novel, *Staying On*, was awarded the Booker Prize, and Carol returned to England to collect it in his stead. Paul's unfashionably hermetic world and the larger literary world had come together at last. Philip Larkin was chairman of the jury.

Meanwhile, learning that Paul's cancer was terminal, Penny, after a year and a half, quietly slipped back into Paul's life, just as he had hoped she would. When Paul came home in December, Penny and his daughters were there to greet him, and for a little over three months they were a real family. Paul died on March 1, 1978.

PAUL SCOTT: A Life by Hillary Spurling. New York, Norton, 1991.

Fictional Space: John Keeble

John Keeble has written a thrilling book. It is also one of the first major novels to be situated in the Northwest. A thrilling book which is not merely a "thriller;" a book set in the West which is more, much more, than a Western—no wonder some of the reviewers, though admiring, seemed confused! The average regional novel is so drab it loses me about page four, and I am the kind of reader who is impatient with descriptions of scenery. But when a writer describes Spokane like this, I am with him all the way:

> A natural hollowing of land, a big abundant dish, the place magnetized life and settlement, and the blood of Indian nations and white settlers had flowed here as recently as a hundred years ago. . . . So when passing or coming to Spokane, he always thought . . . some catechism of history, and so then he always wondered when the original magnetism had played out and how it came to be replaced by the hot and centripetal magnetism of the city built on the ancient place.

That's my home town. But I assume that most of you are like me in that you are loyal less to a specific town than to a

146

region. My region extends, roughly, from Vancouver, B.C. through northern California to the Bay, and stretches from mid-Montana and Idaho down through eastern Oregon to the purple hills of Reno. This is the territory of Keeble's book.

Keeble has cunningly made his protagonist, Wesley Erks, an amateur historian of the West—with all the passion for his subject that is implicit in the word "amateur." This enables him, in the most natural way in the world, to present meditations on scenery and history which I find enthralling. As in this scene, outside Rathdrum, Idaho—where a rundown farm houses the finest collection of shiftless, no-'count white trash, comic and macabre, this side of Mr. Faulkner:

> Lewis and Clark had turned circles in the vicinity, searching for the route to the Columbia, turned around three times by the Bitterroots. The tribes here—the Coeur d'Alenes, the Kalispel and Kootenai to the north, and southward the Nez Percé—were proud, 'socially developed,' and, it was said, self-sufficient, savage, slow to relent. Of the transcontinental railroads, the Northern Pacific was the last to push through to the coast. What was to the outside a barrier was on the inside great pressure, the topography physically closing the people off, the country a wild, craggy, hard, volcanic country, the towns—mining towns originally, mostly lumber towns now— built in pockets, ravines, hollows, and up against cliffs, the people insular, and the routes of travel serpentine, following the watersheds. The tribes had traveled according to the seasons north and west to fish, northwest to dig roots, and east to hunt buffalo, and in all directions to trade, but the white people, most of them, displayed an inclination to roost and to let

others occupy the paths of trade, and, thus, the Panhandle made sects as it attracted them, the Amish, the Hutterites, the Waldenses, lately hippies, castaways from the sixties, those who refused, and Satanist cults, those of the darker versions. . . . It was a place where migration— a sense of trade, goods, or ideas—if it was not entirely arrested was inward, impacted, heavy, where visions were wayward and dense, dis- covered like insects under a stone, lifted, or grubs under bark, torn off a tree.

That is so good I can taste it—but beyond the lovely writing it is accurate and incisive, encapsulating so much history, so much atmosphere in a paragraph or two. But beyond this, the book is also, if I may be so quaint, morally thrilling. (The morality of art is a subject which has been conspicuously missing of late.)

Once I delivered a sermon to the inmates of the National Cathedral School for girls. I used for my text William Stafford's poem, *Traveling Through the Dark,* which movingly illustrated the point that choosing between good and bad isn't a real problem; it's choosing between bad and another bad. Keeble's permutations on that theme are far more complex than mine were (but after all he is writing for grown-ups, which puts him in a special category right there). Wesley Erks is a kind of drop-out from what he considers an immoral society; he feels justified, or thinks he does, in dealing outside the law—in running cocaine and illegal immigrants across the Canadian border to San Francisco. What happens in the course of this novel is what might be called the moral education of Wesley Erks.

The long drives over the back roads of British Columbia across the border, and down to Reno and San Francisco, give him time to speculate, meditate, and remember—the first requirement of moral development. He is assisted further by the company of a distinguished, silent and subtle Chinese named Taam, whose native language is a mystery to us, whom Erks is smuggling out of Vancouver, along with three Chinese men (the "yellowfish" of the title). One of the Chinese boys is wounded unto death; they are closely pursued, as if by the hounds of heaven, by another car, or cars, whether enemies or allies is obscure for a long time. In Rathdrum, they take on the relief driver, Lily, wife of a complex scoundrel named Lucas Tenebrel. All along the way, decisions must be made. Does Erks halt, risking all their lives, to find a doctor for the young Chinese who is nearly dead? If you carry out an action which an immoral society deems illegal, to what extent are you corrupted by those to whom the illegal is a way of life—Lucas, Lily, the dealers and gamblers and middlemen of Reno and San Francisco's Chinatown? Was the old wisdom right when it counseled, "Touch pitch and you shall be defiled"?

In an interview in *Spokane Magazine,* Keeble said, "One of the things that was going on in my mind and that I am still working with is that what Erks has done from the outset is to put himself into a situation that is certainly illegal and probably immoral. In the mind of the reader this is going to be seen as a questionable activity. But for Erks that's given. That's the world in which he's going to live in the novel. A world of moral flux. What he does within that world is act with a degree of morality. He treats a possum with respect, he treats his wife with respect, he treats Ho (the young Chinese who dies on the road) with respect. They're all kinds of things he's doing which are really almost stodgy. Erk's morality is a central preoccupation of the book."

Lily Tenebrel is attractive though aging, horny and unscrupulous. There is another moral choice to be made, although of a lesser order. To most Americans, morality is a matter of sexual morality exclusively. It's widely considered to be okay to lie, cheat, and steal to make profits or get elected. But lust is wicked. Wesley is too subtle a customer to entertain

149

this notion—but still he is surprised to learn that wicked Lily has her scruples too. "Brought herself to the verge, she desisted, held back by death and menses, and respect, her sense of his morality and of her capacity for betrayal." Indeed, one of the great themes of the book is how complex we are— what an amalgam of good, bad and indifferent traits; the possibilities which exist in us for getting better or going under—and that part of the moral education of all of us is in our exposure to the various strains of human behavior—so that we judge not, lest we be judged; yet intrinsic to our morality, and our maturity, is that we judge *ourselves* fiercely, that the moral compact we make with ourselves is the most important decision of our lives.

I can't end this inadequate appraisal (the book is so rich; I've hardly touched on the complexities of plot, of persons, of events) without giving you a taste of one of the most splendid women in modern fiction: Wesley's wife, Ruby. Just run through a catalogue of women in American fiction of the twentieth century and try to come up with a robust, believable woman of glory in her maturity. Lolita? One of Saul Bellow's ex-wives? One of Norman Mailer's ex-wives? One of John Updike's nameless jumping-jill sexual athletes? Philip Roth's mother? Here's Ruby, fixing a motorcycle for a subsidiary character, a small sinister creep who takes pot-shots at celebrities:

> She bent over the carburetor and backed out the needle, enriching the mixture, and listened. When the sputter flattened out, she kept turning until it began to choke and almost died, then turned it back quickly, and rolled the needle slowly to and fro until she found dead center, the heart of the sound, a pulse as tangible as heartbeat. She looked up. "Now rev it."

He gave it a little gas.

"Gun the fucker!" She stood and shoved his hand off the throttle and unwound it until the engine roared, blanking out all sound of wind. The engine had a wobble, a large undulation of sound. "Hold it" she shouted.

He did so, but at arm's length and wincing at the noise.

She went to work on the main jet. She knew about this, main and low-speed jets. The rest of it had been luck. As she backed the needle out, the wobble narrowed to nothing and the roar of the engine was transformed into pure scream which rattled the metal walls of the shop. She stayed on her knees for a moment, listening. The sound made the bones in her head buzz and ran down her back and she felt an ache in her legs. She rose, swaying slightly. They were surrounded by a fog of blue exhaust.

"Damn!" she said, taken by her success. "I'll be damned!"

He mouthed the word: "What?"

She pushed his hand off the throttle. The engine burbled down to idle. She goosed the engine, let it drop back, and goosed it again. The whine arched gracefully. When she switched the cycle off, it was as if the floor of the building had dropped fifty feet into the ground and briefly the sound of the wind was airy, decorative. She felt light.

Disappointed, he said, "That's remarkable."

With the work, half her hair had fallen free of the scarf and she had a grease smudge on her cheek. Her face glowed. She looked strong enough to break the spine of a large dog across her knee.

Through her competence, she gets rid of him. Strong woman.

Well, if that doesn't fetch you, I give up. As you may have gathered by now, I want you to read this book, cherish it, lend it to your friends . . . All the things that you have thought and felt about our particular world are here expressed. Oddly enough, you will feel, as I do, that somehow you helped write it.

Yellowfish, by John Keeble. New York, Harper and Row, 1978.

In the Skin of a Lion:
Michael Ondaatje

Like most normal readers when handed a novel by a poet, or a work described as written in "poetic prose," I usually drop it like a live coal. However, that would be an error in the case of "In the Skin of a Lion," whose author, Michael Ondaatje, is a brilliantly gifted poet and memoirist. Central to his story is the life and character of Patrick Lewis, who as a lad learns from his logger father how to clear logjams with dynamite, and who grows up to use high explosives to express his hatred of the wretched conditions of working men and women in the Toronto of the 1920's.

An orderly and linear account of Patrick's youth this is not. So that the reader isn't put off by the frequent and sometimes lengthy divagations into the lives of seemingly unconnected characters, he or she should ponder well an epigraph by John Berger, the British Marxist art critic and novelist, at the opening of this tale: "Never again will a single story be told as though it were the only one." Mr. Ondaatje manages to pick up most of the loose threads in his complex tapestry by the time the book winds down. Not all of them. Crucial events go unexplained; characters who seem important at the time disappear without a trace. Other characters are scantily identified, if at all. (Briffa, who the devil was Briffa? I read the book three times and am still mystified.) It's like life itself.

The novel is a story—or more accurately stories—told to a young girl by Patrick as he drives north to rendezvous with an old mistress, one of the two great passions of his life. People who are fussy about academic niceties such as "point of view" are not going to be entirely happy with this book. They will take irritable note of the number of times scenes take place or emotions are expressed about which the protagonist could have no knowledge. I have a feeling Mr. Ondaatje knows all this perfectly well and doesn't care. Born in Sri Lanka when it was Ceylon, he was educated and grew up in England and Canada. This book more closely resembles the writing that is being done on the Continent these days: episodic, fragmentary, structurally loose and shifty. And he's a beautiful writer.

What he writes about most beautifully is work. Mr. Ondaatje is passionate about process, the way work, particularly construction of all kinds, is done and how it feels to do it. This is, of course, a rarity in fiction at any time, and one can only be grateful for a man who is not focused on the classroom, the bedroom and the bar.

> Nicholas Temelcoff is famous on the bridge,
> a daredevil. He is given all the difficult jobs and
> he takes them. He descends into the air with
> no fear. He is a solitary. He assembles ropes,
> brushes the tackle and pulley at his waist, and
> falls off the bridge like a diver over the edge of
> a boat. The rope roars alongside him, slowing
> with the pressure of his half-gloved hands. He
> is burly on the ground and then falls with
> terrific speed, grace, using the wind to push
> himself into corners of abutments so he can
> check driven rivets, sheering valves, the dry-
> ing of the concrete under bearing plates and
> padstones. He stands in the air banging the
> crown pin into the upper cord and then shep-
> herds the lower cord's slip-joint into position.
> Even in archive photographs it is difficult to

find him. Again and again you see vista before you and the eye must search along the wall of sky to the speck of burned paper across the valley that is him, an exclamation mark, somewhere in the distance between bridge and river: He floats at the three hinges of the crescent-shaped steel arches. These knit the bridge together.

There is an extraordinary episode in which five nuns walk out onto the unfinished bridge in the dark, toward the fires of the workmen. The wind flings them against the cement mixers and steam shovels; the workmen grab some of them and hang on but one nun is blown over the bridge. Nicholas catches her before she can fall into the water, ripping his arm out of its socket. The entire scene and its aftermath in the Ohrida Lake Restaurant, where the nun and Nicholas drink brandy, then she sits beside him all the night as he sleeps, is a gorgeous set piece and lives on in the reader's eye.

After he comes to Toronto, Patrick gets a job as a "searcher." Men are paid $4 a week, in 1921, to look for a missing millionaire named Ambrose Small. We are told that "gradually [Patrick] came into contact with Small's two sisters," without a word of explanation of how a young workman from the woods pulls off this feat. They tell him to look up Clara Dickens, Small's mistress, in Paris, Ontario. Patrick and Clara become lovers almost immediately. "He was drawing out her history with Small, a splinter from a lady's palm." In the course of this we come to my favorite line of dialogue: "'Would it be forgivable to say I stayed with him because he gave me a piano?'"

But there seems to be a good deal more to the relationship than this: Clara knows where Small is, and goes to him, abandoning her obsessed young lover. She does leave him a souvenir, however: a live iguana. (I had thought iguanas required a hot climate definitely not like Toronto, but so what? I guess he is an emblem of the ugly Small.) In the most preposterous episode in the book, Patrick figures out where

Clara and Small are and pursues Clara. Small answers the door and tells Patrick he will go get Clara. Instead, this millionaire, who presumably commands the services of numberless minions, pours kerosene on Patrick from the roof and drops a match on him. Patrick runs for his life and jumps in a pool, whereupon Small throws something like a Molotov cocktail at him and nearly blinds him.

The next day Clara visits Patrick at the hotel and finds him bruised, blood-covered, one-eyed and cut up. And we have my second-favorite bit of dialogue, also by Clara: "It would be terrible if we met under perfect conditions. Don't you think?" And despite these imperfect conditions, they of course make love.

Many more astounding adventures and surreal episodes lie ahead. I trust that the author doesn't mind a little gentle teasing on the part of the reviewer. I am keeping in mind what Mr. Ondaatje says in rebuttal: "All his life Patrick Lewis has lived beside novels and their clear stories. Authors accompanying their heroes clarified motives. World events raised characters from destitution. The books would conclude with all wills rectified and all romances solvent." And who, these days, wants to write, or read, another neat novel like that?

Finally, one is left remembering the descriptions of work and men at work: Caravaggio, a professional thief, at work; Nicholas Temelcoff, not only building bridges and rescuing nuns but becoming again what he once was, a baker; Patrick tunneling under Lake Ontario and laying his charges of dynamite; Patrick working in a tannery, where the men's knives "weaved with the stride of their arms and they worked barefoot as if walking up a muddy river, slicing it up into tributaries." And the desperate hardships and terrible exploitation of the workingmen, which led to injuries, deaths, desperation and anarchism. If you don't read this book by Mr. Ondaatje— and I urge you to do so—be sure to read the next one.

In the Skin of a Lion, by Michael Ondaatje, New York, Knopf, 1987.

Theodore Roethke
as Teacher

Back in the 'seventies, when I was teaching at Chapel Hill, this outfit in Florida had the brilliant idea of tape-recording people who had studied with distinguished poet-teachers. They asked me if I would talk about Roethke, and I said yes. They sent me big reels of tape; they had acquired a studio in Raleigh, and they'd gone to all manner of trouble to set this up; but the more I thought about it the more frozen I got. Time went on, and I hadn't done anything; I started getting anxious phone calls from Florida, and finally they said, "Ms. Kizer, are you going to do this or aren't you?" And I said, "Well, you know, it's too raw; it's too fresh in my mind, his death, and I haven't been able to handle it yet." There was a silence, and the guy at the other end of the phone said, "Do you realize that Theodore Roethke has been dead for thirteen years?" And I said, "No. No, I don't." And this is one of the first times I've really tried to talk about Ted and what his teaching methods were like. I may say that when I go back and look at my notebooks from those days in his class of '55–'56 (and whenever I could get a chance to sit in after that), I'm amazed that my own teaching methods are such a duplicate of his. I'm fascinated by the fact that I really haven't thought up anything much on my own. I've simply carried on as the master taught me.

That first class in '55 was an extraordinary class; in it were

James Wright, Jack Gilbert, and a man who's now a distinguished German scholar, and head of his university department, named Helmut Bonheim. There was also a seventy-year-old rabbi; a man even older than that who was a retired sea captain, who had just lost his wife and was beside himself with boredom and pain; and people of eighteen. It was the whole spectrum. Ted always insisted on having a class that was open to the public. You didn't have to have any credentials to be in it, you just went and talked to him and he decided whether or not you should be in the class. And so you had a wonderful mix of all kinds of people of all ages, from kids to grandparents.

One of the very striking things about Roethke was his attitude toward these old men in the class. He could be a real brute, particularly when drinking. He was the original male chauvinist pig. But with the rabbi and with the sea captain he was charmingly deferential because, he said, they knew things the rest of us didn't know. They knew what life was like and they had a *subject*. And both these men, the sea captain in particular, contributed a good deal to the class.

When Jim Wright came to class, "we knew at once he was our genius," to quote a poem of mine. Jim came from Kenyon College; he was writing brilliantly, and was well into the work on his first book, *St. Judas*. Jack and I were not that far along, and I probably doubted if we ever would be. But there was an atmosphere in that classroom that is unlike anything I've ever come across. Whenever I get a chance to have an open class like that I do it, because it is an invaluable experience to have a cross-section of people by age and occupation, and even by talent. Experience has its own contribution to make, and Ted was always very conscious of that.

The great thing about Ted was that he knew how to make a good poem out of a bad poem. I was one of those instinctive writers—I think Gilbert was the same way—who would write a poem and ask a couple of people what they thought, and if it wasn't any good we'd throw it away. When I was at Sarah

158

Lawrence I had Horace Gregory for one class. I was in my Robert Frost period—the war was on then, World War II—and I'd written a poem about a woman whose son had died at sea; his body was not recovered. So she took the cradle she had woven for him out to the backyard and buried it. I turned in the poem and Horace Gregory didn't object to the Frost influence, but I had farm animals in the poem, particularly pigs, and Gregory said, "Pigs are not poetic." So I left that class and never went back.

Then I had Genevieve Taggard as my advisor and Genevieve would look at a poem and say, "Darling, this is wonderful. Send it to *The New Yorker*." Or, "Darling, this isn't wonderful," and drop it in the wastebasket. And I didn't have a clue about how you made a good poem out of a bad poem for nearly a decade, until I caught up with Ted.

That was Roethke's great gift. I like to think that it has become mine too, over the years. I'm not interested in that sort of perfect Iowa Workshop poem, in which everything eccentric or outrageous has been ironed out: one of those neat little poems that is disposable like Kleenex: you read it once (though you may not finish it) and think, "Very nice," and then you never think about it again. But I can take a great big messy ambitious poem and find its form and help to shape it up.

Ted said many useful things about that kind of poem. One of them was to think of a poem as a three-act play, where you move from one impulse to the next, and then there is a final breath, which is the summation of the action of the whole. He had picked up that wonderful phrase from Sir John Davies which he used in a poem: "She taught me turn, and counter-turn, and stand." Which is the essence of dramatic structure. It's what a long poem has to do. It doesn't require physical action, but there has to be some mental or emotional action that carries through in the poem.

Roethke was an extraordinarily rigorous critic, and if you couldn't take it you didn't learn much. For example, he said the real test was that every line of a poem should be a poem. That's about as tough as you can get. I apply that to my own work and sometimes just throw up my hands. But I find it's extremely useful in getting rid of connectives, passive constructions, surplus adjectives and words that don't have any particular energy in them.

He was fanatic about active verbs. He used to give us lists of verbs from seventeenth-century poets, particularly Vaughan, and say "How many of these can you incorporate in a poem?" He intensely disliked participles. I remember that one time, as I was sedulously following him, I made my speech to a class about passive constructions and a smart student said, "What about 'To be or not to be'?" I said, "Well, that explains Hamlet's nature: his ambivalence, his uncertainty—his basic passivity," and I got out of that one! In another class somebody said, "What about 'Turning and turning in the widening gyre'?" (I've had some smart—and smart-ass—students!) I replied, "When you can write as well as Yeats you won't need to be in this class." But in general those are good practices.

Another thing Ted used to have us do—which I often do with students—is tell them, "Take out all the adjectives and see what you've got left. See which ones are absolutely essential to the poem." It's amazing how poems are improved. Sometimes when they're pared down like that, they speak wonderfully to you. This again was part of his obsession and fascination with the seventeenth century. People like Herbert and Donne and Vaughan use very few adjectives. The whole strength of the poem rests on the verb. The verb is the great armature around which the language of the poem is wrapped, as I've said many times.

Sometimes he would say arbitrarily, "Cut a line out of each stanza," if he felt the poem was a little flaccid, a little loose. So you'd have to conflate two or three lines to make this work. Most times, even when we didn't think it would work, it did. Ted would also ruthlessly cut stanzas that he thought were not on the main track of the poem. The first poem of mine that was widely anthologized was a poem about the death of my mother called "The Great Blue Heron." Ted took two stanzas out of it. It was because I trusted him so much that I agreed to do this, although I felt like an amputee. Within two months I couldn't even remember what was missing. He pointed out something to me that I have noticed all my life since, and that is when you take out a big hunk of a poem, the part that comes before and the part that comes after the cut just seal up, including the rhymes, as if you had discovered the poem's true form, the form the poem had been trying to make you understand all the time.

I had a brilliant student one time when I carried the Roethke cut to extremes. She had a poem in eight-line stanzas and I made her take a line out of each stanza; each day she took out another line, and we had it down to quatrains! And the poem got better each day. She was a good sport about it, and had a wonderful professional attitude. She saw what happened when this whole process of condensation took place. I've never had the courage to be that drastic with anybody else; but because this was a strong person who had such a strong motivation, I felt I could say something like this to her without tearing her up.

Roethke was very concerned with trying other forms when a poem wasn't working particularly well. He'd say, "Put it in triplets, try it in couplets," and "The thing about these shorter stanzas is they leave a lot of white space, and you can see if those lines will stand up by themselves." When you write a long, dense poem and you haven't bothered to make stanzas or you've got long shapeless stanzas, you can get away with a lot. Whitman got away with a lot. Ginsberg does. In a forest of verbiage, you can't see clearly enough to deploy intellectual rigor to the lines.

Just about as difficult as saying that every line of a poem should be a poem was, "Read down the first words in each line and see if they make a kind of poem; if they're nothing but 'and,' 'but,' 'so,' 'thus,' 'maybe,' then try to make the first

161

word of each line interesting." I could open a book of Ted's almost at random and take the first word of each line: "on," "kingdom," "fetter," "worst," "saliva," "agony," "lust," "how," "dreams," "bleak," "great," "not." See how close that is to being a poem?

Other pieces of his good advice: "If you find you have great facility in something, work against it." He noticed that I rhymed with ease, so he warned me against too many perfect rhymes, and too many end-rhymes. "Bury them in the line!" he said. And I've done that. One must always try to do what one can't do, not what one can do already.

When it came to editing the poem, Ted would say, "Any fool can cut a bad line. It takes a real pro to cut a good line." But how we cling to those good lines which are just salad-dressing, irrelevant, or which don't advance the movement of the poem! So we play a little game when we cut out the goodies; we tell ourselves that we'll put them in another poem. Sometimes these lines *do* provide the impetus for another poem, like starter for sourdough. But usually they just keep traveling from poem to poem. You can cannibalize a car far more easily than you can a poem.

But the most important thing Roethke ever said was after class when another student was very critical of some eccentric thing I had done, and Ted admonished him, "You want to be very careful when you criticize something like that because it may be the hallmark of an emerging style." He knew that our eccentricities are part of our true voice. And he was a great deal more disciplined than people who didn't know him give him credit for. I believe he wrote every day—wrote and read and made notes in an ever-increasing pile of notebooks. It was from these voluminous notebooks that David Wagoner assembled *Straw for the Fire*, a fascinating and neglected book. Ted would put down a little phrase here and a little phrase there, and brood about them. One of the reasons he sometimes plagiarized was that he didn't always take note of who had said what. In my own notebooks, I am careful to put down the attribution, and if it's some brilliant thing I thought up myself I put "CK" after it!

Although, as I've said, Ted was this ferocious male chauvinist in private life (the women in class put up with stuff that women today wouldn't dream of enduring. We used to joke that we would buy girdles so that we couldn't have our butts pinched with such ease; and after two drinks he'd think nothing of plunging his index finger down between your breasts). But in class he was somebody else. The people he loved to quote from were women poets. Louise Bogan. Leonie Adams. The obscure English poet Ruth Pitter, who died last year at the age of 95. I can still hear Ted reciting her poem:

> "But for lust we could be friends.
>   On each others' necks, could weep:
> In each other's arms could sleep
>   In the calm the cradle lends:
> Lends awhile and takes away.
>   But for hunger, but for fear,
> Calm could be our day and year
>   From the yellow to the grey:
>
> From the gold to the grey hair . . .

I know it all by heart. Ted was very big on memorization. "There will be times in your life," he used to say in his growly voice, "when you will be trapped. You won't have anything to read, you'll be in the line at the supermarket, you'll be sitting in the dentist's office, and if you've got those poems in your head, it's not just that they will help you with your work, they will help you through the dry times in your life." And they do. But it's hard to get students to memorize poems. Most of them are very resistant.

The following year, I studied with Stanley Kunitz. That was very interesting, because Ted was the intuitive teacher. My volume of the collected William Butler Yeats has Ted's comments on the left-hand margin and Stanley's comments on the right-hand margin. If Ted wanted to know anything about a reference—research about Madam Blavatsky, or Georgie Yeats, or anything that Yeats might have done or said—he assigned us the tasks of finding out. Stanley, on the other hand, had read every book in Yeats' library, and catalogued the poems and cross-catalogued them, so that we got Yeats from both directions, those of us who were lucky enough to be in both classes.

But I brought up Stanley because, again, he was somebody that I found very necessary to memorize. I memorized a lot of Roethke and I can say, oh, ten or fifteen poems of his. When I began reading Kunitz, I'd be upstairs, and a couple of lines of a poem would come into my head and I couldn't remember the next line, so I'd get out of bed, put on my dressing gown, get on my slippers, walk down the stairs, get Stanley's book, check out the next line, close the book, put it back on the shelf, and go upstairs, take off my robe and slippers, get back into bed. Finally I said, the hell with this—I'm going to learn the poems so I don't have to go through this ridiculous process.

I think Bogan's tracks are quite easy to follow in Ted's early poems. For example, "Thought does not crush to stone. / The great sledge drops in vain. / Truth never is undone; / Its shafts remain." That's just Bogan all over the place. And so in a way is, "My secrets cry aloud. / I have no need for tongue," the first poem in *Open House.* You must read the correspondence between Roethke and Bogan; you have to get Louise's letters to read that. It is just wonderful. They had this extraordinary love affair. He was twenty-seven and she was forty-two, something like that. And they had this rampageous, violent, and drunken affair about which Louise wrote divinely to Ralph Humphries and Morten Dowen Zabel. They're touching and hilarious. It was very tough for Louise because of the age difference and she, as I have said sometimes, was a kind of menopausal poet. She felt old when she was young. But they managed to combine this love affair with a wonderful exchange of advice about their poems. They taught each other a great deal, and she ended up being his Best Woman when he got married to Beatrice O'Connell. The people who stood up with him were Louise Bogan and W. H. Auden; that's pretty grand.

One of the things that he talked a lot about with Louise was the way she began poems with a prepositional phrase: "Beyond the hour we counted rain that fell . . .," "Under the thunder-dark, the cicadas resound . . .," "Over our heads, if we but knew . . ." At least a dozen poems, some of Louise's very best poems, begin with a prepositional phrase. What's the virtue of that? You're plunged into the middle of the poem. There's no winding up. There's no setting of the stage, no description of fields, and trees, and poppies, and emotional states, and so on. You're right there.

Louise was an interesting case in many ways. She wrote almost nothing in the last thirty years of her life, partly because she was the poetry editor of *The New Yorker*, which she should have quit long before she did. But part of it I think was this idea of feeling like an old woman when she was in her thirties. One time in my living room Kunitz was there with Louise, and Louise was probably fifty-two or something like that. She said, "Oh I wish I knew a nice woman to go to Europe with." And Kunitz said, "Hell, Louise, why don't you go with a man?" And she drew back and said, "Oh Stanley!" as if that were the most outrageous thing she had ever heard. She was still a very handsome woman, very good-looking, good figure, fair hair with a black velvet band around it which she always wore. But somehow she blocked. I think part of it was being someone who should have been a feminist and couldn't quite bring herself to be. The Irish in her got in the way, I think. She wrote wonderful poems, like "Medusa" or "Cassandra," with a mythological mask, because she was unable to talk directly about herself. Instead of saying, "I don't want to be a mother," she put it in the mouth of Cassandra. If she wanted to express a sense of stasis, of being frozen, she disguised herself as Medusa. Nowadays, of course, people

165

come right out with it (sometimes they come out with too much of it as far as I'm concerned), but I don't think Roethke ever balked at being open and free. But then he was a man; it was easier for him.

Leonie Adams is one of the most neglected modern figures, partly because she's a pure lyric poet, partly because she's not only lyric, she's metaphysical and she's difficult. I would like to see Leonie brought back into prominence, because she was a lovely poet and a lovely human being.

Ted stole freely from Kunitz. Stanley never complained about this or even mentioned it. Ted stole from me. I have a poem, "Hera, Hung From the Sky," which ends, "I dangle drowned in fire," a line which Ted instantly stole, and as he was quite famous and I was quite unknown, I took it downtown and had it notarized with the date on which I wrote it! I wanted to make it plain I got there first!

I recently edited *The Essential John Clare*. It was his two hundredth birthday in 1993, and I have been giving readings of his poems. Mine is the first American edition of Clare's work. Clare was a great nature poet, and a great lyric poet, and a man whose greatest virtue was his infinite power of observation. He could lie on the grass for four or five hours waiting for a mama bird to come back to her nest. His poems about birds always describe the eggs—their shape, their size, their color, how many there were. Very precise. Rather like Jean Henri Fabre writing about the life of the bee. He was very concerned to get it right. He was a beautiful poet. And when I read Clare's poem "The Badger," I can hear Roethke's voice reading it. He had this rather deep growly voice, and this poem is full of wonderful plosives, powerful monosyllables, and they relentlessly pound away at you. Technically it's an extraordinary poem, and Ted relished every beat of it. But I think other than Kunitz, Yeats and Clare, I can't remember other male poets that he used to quote in class, oddly enough. He certainly never quoted any of his contemporaries, other than Kunitz, who was then largely unknown, although fifty-ish. Lowell and Jarrell were very much presences. I think there was an element of competition there; but Ted felt very strongly that you need to learn from your seniors rather than your contemporaries. I remember him saying something to the effect that you would be too influenced by the mannerisms of those poets, which might be exactly the things that made them fade from view. He liked to go back to the seventeenth century, as Clare did. He skipped happily over the nineteenth century, and most of the eighteenth, to where the English language was fresh and precise.

We used to have long conversations about punctuation. At one point my ex-husband had a tap on my telephone. He was trying to take my children away from me and had hired a detective to monitor phone calls. Stanley or Ted and I were saying things like, "In the fourth line I took out that comma that used to be there . . ." And the next day, "No, I took out the semi-colon and put the comma back in." The detective must have thought we were talking in code! Ah, for poets punctuation and money are the great topics!

One of Ted's great attributes as a teacher is that none of us who studied with him write at all like Roethke. If Ted caught any of us imitating him we never did it again. He would tease us mercilessly. Hugo and Wagoner were students of Ted before our group, and after us came Sandra McPherson and Tess Gallagher. I can always spot a Hugo student. I was in Buffalo, I think, and a girl showed me a poem in class and I said, "When did you study with Richard Hugo?" and she was absolutely floored. "How did you know?" Dick had a set of rules, which I've been trying for years to get a copy of, which guaranteed that you would write a Richard Hugo poem. We always made excuses for Hugo, he was insecure, and was comforted by followers. Well, Ted was insecure too, but he didn't do that.

Bill Matthews has said that a really good writing teacher wants you to write more and more like yourself, while a less good teacher wants you to write like him or her—only slightly less well! It's almost guaranteed that if you're imitating somebody else it will be less good—which is not to say that you shouldn't experiment by imitating others, but that these experiments should be confined to your notebook. I was speaking recently to a friend whose son is in love with Eliot, Auden and Merrill. My admiration for Jim Merrill is unbounded. But this young man is inhibited and controlled; he needs to be crazier. And here he's sedulously imitating Jim's carefully crafted stanzas with those wonderful rhymes. It's all wrong for him. Annie Finch sent me her manuscript the other day, and when I'd read it I said, "I know now why you write such formal poetry. It's because you're quite mad. You use form to contain your madness."

People like that are a lot more fun to teach. Let me have students and friends who are excessive, emotionally excessive—and maybe a little crazy too! I used to say to students, "Bring me your tired, your poor, your struggling iambs yearning to breathe free." Then I can go to work and help find a formal structure or a dramatic structure on which to drape all the craziness. Who really wants to read a perfect poem by a young poet? When I first came across the poems of Ed Hirsch I thought, "Wow! Here is all this feeling, this energy, this nuttiness! Wonderful." Hirsch keeps getting better and better without losing that fine edge of craziness. And I have a deep weakness for the poetry of Bill Knott as well.

Of course Roethke really was crazy, in the clinical sense, so poetry was a life-and-death matter for him. He was a manic-depressive (mis-diagnosed for years as a schizophrenic), and at the high end of the spectrum he wrote bad poetry, and in the low end he couldn't write at all, so he had to catch the muse in the periods in between. A lot of nonsense has been written about Ted as crazy all the time or drunk all the time. I picked up an English literary magazine the other day—the English always get us wrong, you know—where someone said that Roethke wrote some of his best poems when he was drunk. Nobody writes a good poem when he's drunk, with the possible exception of Patrick Kavanagh!

One thing really irritates me about recent biographies of Ted, Robert Lowell, John Berryman, Anne Sexton and others: they all drank; they all had episodes of mental instability, but in these biographies they are made to seem drunk or crazy all the time. These were people who met their classes, taught their students, wrote their work with steady brilliance. But these biographers string the lurid episodes together as if they were the life. They weren't, they aren't, and they never will be.

I saw Ted drink a lot, but rarely drunk. His guests were more often drunk than he. I remember parties in his garden in the summer, in Seattle: very hot and humid. Ted would be wandering around with a large martini pitcher, topping off your drink at frequent intervals, and because you had lost count of how much you had consumed, you had drunk seven martinis, and were reeling.

Many poets drank a lot before a reading, always a stressful event no matter how many times they've done it, so perhaps this contributed to the perception that they were drunks. And in some cases there may have been mental episodes which looked like drunkenness but which were illness.

Two great events in Ted's life after I got to know him—aside from the major breakdowns—were, first, the death of Dylan Thomas. This was a great shock to him, and caused him to think long, long thoughts about reforming. As a result, he seriously tried to cut down on his drinking and roistering, and committed himself firmly to heterosexuality. (How seriously his erotic forays in this department were can only be speculated upon; I suspect it was mainly boastful talk.) The second great thing was when he met and married Beatrice O'Connell, which further stabilized his life and which resulted in the greatest love poems since Yeats. Beatrice was a great beauty. Not one of our leading brains by any means. But so decorative, so quiet, such a great cook! What every man wants! And there was this outpouring of magnificent poems: "I knew a woman, lovely in her bones . . ." and those "memorable lines" ("Quote me a memorable line," I've heard Ted say dozens of times.) from "Words for the Wind":

> "Passion's enough to give
> Shape to a random joy:
> I cry delight: I know
> The root, the core of a cry.
> Swan-heart, arbutus-calm,
> She moves when time is shy:
> Love has a thing to do . . .
>
> Under the rising moon;
> I smile, no mineral man;
> I bear, but not alone,
> The burden of this joy."

A whole series of ravishing poems that one cannot read or re-read without tears. But as Ted grew older, between bouts of mental illness that occurred increasingly often, he began to think more and more about death, so much so that his death was a shock, but not a surprise. But these meditations led to poems like "In a Dark Time," one of the great poems in the language.

Some people have a difficult time with the poems of his middle period that use what Roethke called "pre-verbal" material, or the nursery-rhyme cadences that occur in "The Lost Son" and other poems of that period. Re-reading the poem I'm struck by how heavily spondaic it is, spondee after spondee: Listen to them: "dead cry," "slow drip," "soft-sigh," "hard time," "old wound," "one fly"—all these in the first nineteen lines. I used to have a theory—I may still—that you could tell a natural-born poet from the outset by the instinctive use of spondees.

Throughout the poem the poet asks questions, a very effective device. It brings the reader right into the poem, a participant: "Tell me / Which is the way I take: / Out of what door do I go, / Where and to whom?" Then he makes frequent use of the pathetic fallacy, not just to try to animate forms in nature, but to reveal mental unease, a man talking to a tree. Then he moves into nursery rhyme or skip-rope rhyme cadences: "The shape of a rat? / It's bigger than that. / It's less than a leg / And more than a nose, / Just under the water / It usually goes." I'll say more about these cadences in a minute, but first I want to mark the entrance of James Joyce. You will find echoes of, or parallels with, *Portrait of the Artist as a Young Man* throughout: the image of the rat under the water, symbol of adolescent sexual anxiety. The passage in Part 3: "From the mouths of jugs / Perched on many shelves, / I saw substance flowing / That cold morning." Right out of *Portrait* . . . ! Whether consciously or not, who can say? How little we know about the common experiences of sensitive alienated children!

To get back to the skip-rope rhymes: Ted admitted freely that he was influenced by Iona and Peter Opie, husband and wife, who hung around children's playgrounds in England and listened to their games. They prove that many of their rhyming games go way back in time: jokes about, say, King Charles and his mistress are handed down and updated to jokes about the Prince of Wales, the earlier one, and Mrs. Simpson. (I suppose now there are jokes about the present Prince of Wales and his Camilla.) None of this material had been written down till the Opies came along. A pure example of the last remaining vestiges of the oral tradition—from Homer to hop-scotch! Ted was fascinated by the oral tradition, and used its mnemonic devices for what may be the first time in modern poetry. Other poets have since become concerned with what you might call Ur-poetry. As Bill Matthews has said, reading it is like getting to know diamonds when they are still leaves.

But I'd like to speak a bit about the over-all structure of the poem. It's useful to regard it as if it were a Noh play. In the Noh, the principal characters are ghosts, and the action of the play is a flashback. They are in limbo, and are trying to ascend to a higher state of consciousness by achieving self-knowledge. They acquire understanding by re-living the past. This is what Roethke is doing, in symbolic language, until he gets to Part 4, "The Return", which is straight autobiography. That tyrannical old German, Otto Roethke, makes his appearance with the words "Pipe-knock," standing on a single line. Then, "Scurry of warm over small plants. / Ordnung! ordnung! / Papa is coming!" "Pipe-knock" of course is a wonderful double: the father is knocking his pipe against a pipe which heats the famous Roethke greenhouse. And the pipe itself knocks!

There is another way of looking at the poem: Stanley Kunitz once said that the shape of any poem can be described in symbols: a circle, two sides of a triangle, up-side and down-side, and so on. A striking example of a down-side or avalanche shape is Hopkins' "The Leaden Echo and the Golden Echo", where the poem goes down to the basement of the soul with the lines, "Be beginning to despair, to despair / Despair, despair, despair, despair". Then, with the single word, "Spare!" alone on the next line, the poem begins its ascent. Ted surely learned from this as both poets learned from Dante.

Roethke's poem shows the flight of the madman down into the depths. Part 2 is called "The Pit." Part 3 is "The Gibber:" Nature is against him, the weeds, the snakes, the cows and briars tell him, "Die." The line, "Look, look, the ditch is running white" is a final echo of Joyce; like the water in the jug overflowing, a masturbatory image. Then comes Part 4, "The Return" where the poem begins its ascent, structurally very similar to Hopkins, and ends with "It was beginning winter", where the poem achieves increasing sanity and calm: "The weeds stopped swinging. / The mind moved, not alone, / Through the clear air, in the silence." An exhausted kind of peace, but questioning still. The poem takes on a metaphysical resonance at the end—Eliotic if you will—where the poet asks a series of short questions; and then come the final lines: "A lively understandable spirit / once entertained you. / It will come again. / Be still. / Wait." And the poet awaits a spiritual re-birth. Let's leave Ted there: expectant, and tranquil, as I hope his spirit is.

The font used in the body text of *Picking and Choosing* is Veljovic Book, 11 point with 13.2 point leading.